SS-WIKING

SS-WIKING

THE HISTORY OF THE FIFTH SS DIVISION 1941–45

Rupert Butler

CASEMATE
HAVERTOWN, PA

ISBN 1-932033-04-1

Editorial and design by
Amber Books Ltd
Bradley's Close
74–77 White Lion Street
London N1 9PF

Project Editor: Charles Catton
Editor: David Norman
Design: Mike Rose
Picture Research: Chris Bishop and Lisa Wren

Printed and bound in Italy by: Eurolitho S.p.A., Cesano Boscone (MI)

Extracts from the interviews with Ornulf Bjornstad and Olaf Lindvig,
former members of SS *Wiking*, are reproduced with the permission of the
Sound Archives of the Imperial War Museum, London.

Contents

NEDERLANDERS
VOOR UW EER EN GEWETEN
OP ! - TEGEN HET BOLSJEWISME
DE WAFFEN SS ROEPT U !

CHAPTER ONE

FOUNDATION

Faced with a severe manpower shortage, the *Waffen-SS* sought volunteers from countries occupied by the Germans, including men from the Netherlands, France, Denmark and Norway, to form the future *Wiking* Division, a title intended to embody the ideal of Nordic racial purity.

Allegations of collaboration in World War II can still act as raw nerves on the conscience of nations. Palatable or not, the truth is that thousands of willing youngsters from subjugated countries served Nazi Germany in the various echelons of the *Waffen-SS* ('Armed SS'). At the outbreak of war, figures were negligible. By its end, foreigners outnumbered native Germans in its ranks. There were many young men who, disillusioned by the helplessness of their governments in the face of defeat, were driven to seek a focus for their lives which they saw as being without purpose.

SS-Obergruppenführer (General) Felix Steiner, who became the first commander of the *Waffen-SS* Division '*Wiking*', wrote that 'all these psychological factors and their concern about the future destiny of their homelands combined at this time to lead a part of the youth to make the decision to enter the German *Wehrmacht* as volunteers.' Of the men themselves, he added: 'They observed the good behaviour and discipline of the German troops and began to make comparisons that did not turn out to be unfavourable for the Germans.' At the immediate post-war Nuremberg trials, a Herr

Left: Soon after the German conquest of Denmark, Norway, Belgium and the Netherlands, appeals went out for foreign recruits to join the *Waffen-SS* in the 'fight against Bolshevism'. This is a Dutch recruiting poster.

Brill, a former *SS-Mann* (pre-war rank of private) in the *Leibstandarte*, who later served in the *Ergänzungs Amt* which enrolled *Waffen-SS* recruits, stated:

'In my office, I read thousands upon thousands of applications for admission. I can say that up to 1939 the enthusiasm for the SS, for its decent and proper conduct, was the main reason for volunteering. The men wanted to do their military service in a clean, modern, élite formation.'

GLITTERING PROMISES

But this told only half the story. The truth was that at a material level, the benefits of working for the SS were often tangible. Pay and allotments for foreigners were comparable with that of the Germans. There were attractive inducements to look to the future once the war had been won, glittering promises of civil service preferment and grants of land. These were motives enough, but there were also those who had an ideological commitment to National Socialism which they felt could best be expressed through service in the SS.

From the German viewpoint, there was a strictly practical reason in planning for a rapid expanse of *Waffen-SS* manpower from outside the *Reich*. There was a severe shortage of personnel due to the *Wehrmacht*'s niggardly release of native German volunteers whom it had recruited and wished to retain for itself. As World

War II grew ever nearer, the SS was compelled to look elsewhere for the personnel to man new field divisions. Whatever the reasons, the courtship of the youth of occupied countries worked well. Heinrich Himmler had every reason to be a wholly satisfied individual. In an address to senior officers at Posen on 4 October 1943, the *Reichsführer-SS* was justified in describing his *Waffen-SS* expansion as 'nothing less than fantastic', achieved 'at an absolutely terrific speed'.

The figures, Himmler declared, spoke for themselves. In 1939, the *Waffen-SS* had consisted solely of 'a few regiments, guard units, 8000 to 9000 strong – that is, not even a division; all in all, 25,000 to 28,000 men at the most.' World War II had scarcely been a year old before that strength had reached nearly 150,000. With a six-fold increase in manpower, the *Waffen-SS* was now established as 'the fourth branch of the *Wehrmacht*'.

Rapid Build-Up

By 1940, the SS stood at four divisions. This history is concerned with *SS-Wiking* Division, the 5th Division, whose personnel during the war comprised not only German nationals but also those of Flemish, Dutch, Danish, Norwegian and Finnish origin.

At first, these divisions had been little more than scattered battalions of the *SS-Verfügungstruppen* ('General Purpose Troops'), or SS-VT, which was later renamed the *Waffen-SS*. Then followed their conversion into regiments, one of which was *Germania*, a future component of the division *SS-Wiking*. The breakdown of the west European or 'Germanic' SS, many of whom swelled the ranks of *Wiking*, is given by George H. Stein in his book *Waffen-SS*, as follows:

'... some 50,000 Dutch (making up the largest group); 40,000 SS men being provided by Belgium, almost evenly divided between Flemings and Walloons; 20,000 from France with Denmark and Norway each producing around 6000 men. Another 1200 came from such countries as Switzerland, Sweden and

Right: The foundation of *SS-Standarte Nordland* – volunteers from Denmark and Norway – was announced on 30 April 1940, followed three months later by *SS-Standarte Westland*, made up of men from the Low Countries.

Left: Himmler saw the recruitment of suitably 'Aryan' or 'Nordic' foreign volunteers as an easy way to expand the *Waffen-SS* at the rate that he required, and without any competition from the *Wehrmacht*.

Luxembourg. The figure of those serving from Finland, the least committed of the *Waffen-SS*, has been put at 1000, but various accounts differ.'

The build-up was fast, all the more remarkable when it is remembered that in the early years of the Weimar Republic, the *Schutzstaffel* (SS – Protection Squad) had been little more than the crude repository for bouncers and street-fighters of the fledgling Nazi party. Its power base had been strengthened irrevocably by the overthrow of a serious rival, the *Sturmabteilung* (SA – Stormtroopers) in a bloody coup – which would later be called 'The Night of the Long Knives' – during the summer of 1934.

HIMMLER'S OBSESSION

The hour from then on belonged to *Reichsführer-SS* Heinrich Himmler. The Munich-born former chicken farmer, son of a secondary schoolmaster looked, with his pebble spectacles and prissily didactic manner, every inch the painfully conscientious, unimaginative clerk destined to languish without promotion in some public service backwater. But it was a mistake to assume that this was the whole man. Concealed underneath the mundane exterior was something else: a dangerous individual who had embraced the pseudo-mystic trappings of the Nazi creed, root and branch.

Himmler saw in the black uniform of his SS the symbol of an imagined earlier Germany of supermen and hunters, men who lived by the dagger, products of a twilight world of ferocious guards, Teutonic knights and lion-hearted heroes. The very choice of the name *Wiking* for an SS division had been seen by many as staking a claim to one of those lands in the northern twilight, a home of pagan gods whose beginnings could be traced in the ancient runes. Carried away by an obsession which was rivalled only his hatred of the ever-proliferating Jews, Himmler even spoke in glowing terms of the day when millions of Germans living in America would be members of the SS.

Above: Members of the *SS-Verfügungstruppen* in 1938. In the early years the *Waffen-SS* was dependent on the *Wehrmacht* for its equipment and uniforms, and SS troops were almost indistinguishable from regular soldiers.

He did not, however, permit his racial preoccupations to interfere with his own ceaseless pursuit of power. This, he realized, was a commodity which had to be shared with Hitler himself who, first and foremost, perceived the SS as both a private army and a personal police force. This was in accordance with the words of the Organization Book of the NSDAP (National Socialist or Nazi Party): 'The original and most important duty of the SS is to serve as the protector of the *Führer.*' But the *Reichsführer-SS* was keen to point out: 'By decree of the *Führer* the sphere of duties has been enlarged to include the external security of the *Reich.*' No further definition of 'external security' was forthcoming then but, despite the vagueness of the phrasing, a future military role clearly seemed to be the intention. This had been confirmed by Hitler as early as 1934: 'It will be necessary in future wars for our SS and police, in their own closed units, to prove themselves at the front in the same way as the army and to make blood sacrifices to the same degree as any other branch of the armed forces.'

CONSCRIPTION INTRODUCED

For existing members of the SS, increasing career opportunities were intended in part as something of a reward for their role during the anti-SA putsch in 1934. The early elements of the *SS-Verfügungstruppen* were three regiments, each containing three battalions, as well as a mortar company and a motorcycle company which were supported by a signals battalion.

A meagre affair, certainly. But how it would shape in the future was indicated when Hitler announced in the Reichstag that conscription would be introduced and the *SS-Verfügungstruppen* would be the recipient of the highest possible standard of training. Two former army officers, Paul Hausser and Felix Steiner, were recruited in order to implement this policy.

The post of inspector of the *SS-Verfügungstruppen* (SS-VT) went to Hausser and with it the rank of *SS-Brigadeführer* (Major-General). Hausser was a career soldier with scant time for Himmler's racial fantasies. His sole concern was turning out rock-hard troops in defence of a modern state. After service in World War I, Hausser had retired with the rank of Lieutenant-General only one year before Hitler came to power. Originally he had thrown in his lot with the SA, but, having survived the bloodbath of 'The Night of the Long Knives', he adroitly changed his rank from *SA-Standartenführer* (Colonel) to the equivalent in the SS.

When it came to actual SS-VT training, *SS-Sturmbannführer* (Major) Felix Steiner, a charismatic personality who had served as a junior artillery officer in World War I, seemed an obvious choice. He too had

spotted what he saw as an opportunity to further himself once the Nazis had secured power. Quitting the army with the rank of Colonel and transferring to the SS, Steiner had no intention of being confined within armed outfits created solely to counter internal unrest. He recalled: 'I was among those who frequently plotted to set up a field force of a rather different nature. In doing this we felt we could thereby contribute to Germany's security in the international sense.'

The main stumbling block, as Hausser saw it, was Himmler himself, whom he came to dismiss as 'an out-and-out policeman of the repressive kind and who had no real idea at all of military matters'. Nevertheless, even the mildest suggestion that the *Reichsführer-SS* was being sidelined could prove a dangerous move; both

Below: A map showing the various countries that provided the bulk of the recruits for the *Wiking* Division and the approximate total number of volunteers for the *Waffen-SS* from each of those states.

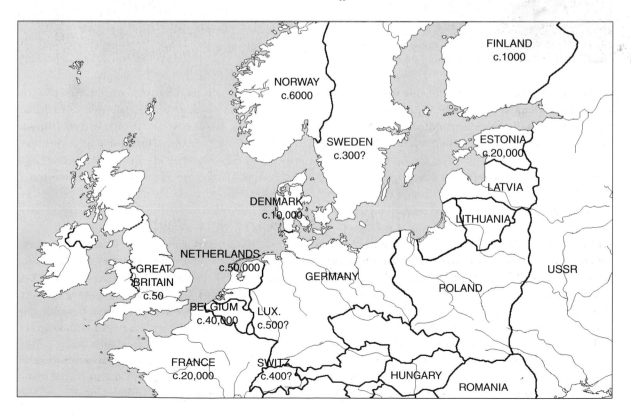

Hausser and Steiner sensed the need to take some of Himmler's prejudices on board. Thus any recruit for the *Waffen-SS,* while allowed some degree of choice as to which branch of service he favoured, had to be between the ages of 17 and 22. Older aspirants were accepted only in exceptional circumstances. Candidates had to 'have an acceptable political outlook' and 'provide evidence of an Aryan origin back to 1800', or even earlier if they were officer candidates.

'ABSOLUTE POWER'

Such stipulations were luxuries that were only practical in time of peace. With the coming of war and a decline in fortunes, strict criteria inevitably became relaxed and eventually were dispensed with altogether. This applied also to foreign 'Germanic' volunteers with height restrictions being lowered to a minimum 1.65m (5ft 5in). The proof of Aryan descent was cut to just two generations. However, this by no means applied to volunteers from some countries who were required to serve the *Waffen-SS* for a fixed term under contract, a source of great relief to those fresh-faced recruits whose sense of idealism withered once they themselves had experienced the horrific privations of fighting on the Eastern Front.

But in one respect, Steiner and Hitler agreed. Here was a great opportunity to demonstrate that whatever the conservative die-hards of the Army could do, the SS could do even better. Given this imprimatur, recruitment for a perceived new and élite force went on apace. In a Germany that had suffered such severe economic privations under the Weimar Republic, the chance of employment and the attendant restoration of national pride were not to be gainsaid. This explained the growth both in stature and in numbers of the SS units which, up to 1936, had been but scattered battalions. At first, its candidates had been a disparate bunch. These men were generally ex-officers from World War I who had nowhere to go, as well as rankers, policemen and plain adventurers, not forgetting the mere hangers-on. From this uneven and often dubious material, Hausser and Steiner hammered into shape the men who would form the officer and NCO cadres of the future *Verfügungstruppen.*

Above: Felix Steiner, the first commander of 5th SS-Division *Wiking*. A revolutionary when it came to training *Waffen-SS* men, Steiner evolved what many observers regarded as the most efficient training system of the war.

By the time of the attack on Poland on 1 September 1939, the men of the SS-VT, who had been shipped to East Prussia, were organized into regimental combat groups. It was after the invasion of western Europe between 10 and 20 May 1940 that Himmler seized the initiative. Beside those engaged in the practicalities of fighting a war, the *Reichsführer-SS* stood as a creature apart. He continued to dream dreams, his major obsession being to attract the purest Nordic blood of Europe into his SS. With his imagination soaring as he poured over his eternal files, he was envisaging what he believed would ultimately become the Germanic province of 'Burgundia', consisting of the

Netherlands, Belgium and north-east France. Germany itself would be protected by this bulwark, with the SS possessing absolute power. In pursuit of this dream, he ensured that members of the *Allegemeine-SS* (General SS) were in place in the captured territories of Flanders, Holland and Norway.

An order went out to General Gottlob Berger, a wily and persuasive Swabian who was head of the SS main leadership office, and a specialist on racial selection for the SS. He was to intensify his efforts to gain foreign recruits for the new *Wiking* Division. It was no easy task. The straight-laced echelons of the *Wehrmacht* were at best unenthusiastic at the prospect of a 'second army' and at worst downright obstructive. The solution lay with Himmler, who happened to hold the post of *Reichskommissar für die Festigung Deutscher Volksturms* (Reich Commissar for the Strengthening of 'Germandom'). With powerful connections among

Germans living abroad, the *Reichsführer-SS* was able to activate contacts over a wide field, thus bypassing normal military restrictions on recruiting abroad. Not least among the advantages of all this for Berger was that such volunteers would not be required to serve in the German Armed Forces. And there was nothing whatever that the *Wehrmacht* could do about it. Western volunteers for the *Waffen-SS* were left in no doubt as to where the power lay, as Himmler made clear:

'Be certain of this. There will be in Europe just one SS – the Germanic-SS under the command of the *Reichsführer-SS*. You can resist, but that is a matter of indifference to me for we will create it in any case. We

Below: Would-be recruits for the *Waffen-SS* were expected to be of the highest physical standard and were subjected to rigid examination. The ideal was a blond, blue-eyed 'Nordic' type, but standards fell as the war progressed.

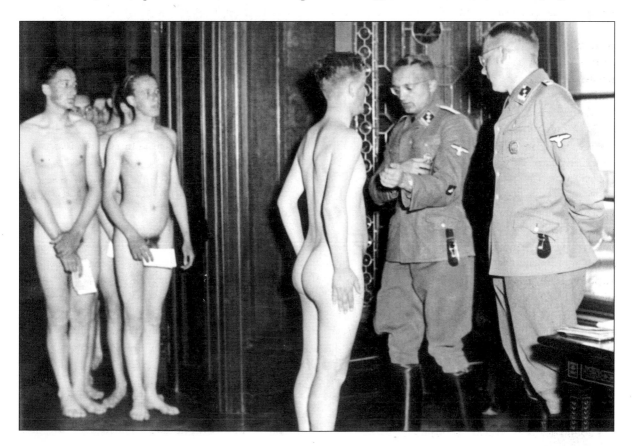

do not ask you to turn against your country, nor to do anything repugnant to anyone proud of his country, who loves it and has his self-respect. Neither do we expect you to become Germans out of opportunism. What do we ask is that you subordinate your national ideal to a superior racial and historical ideal, that of the single and all-embracing Germanic Reich.'

NEW REGIMENTS

With the formation of *Wiking*, which was one of the leading foreign divisions of the *Waffen-SS*, *SS-Gruppenführer* (Lieutenant-General) Felix Steiner became its first commander. There were two new regiments, *Nordland* (consisting of Danes and Norwegians) and *Westland* (Flemish and Dutch). The new division was at first called *Germania* but, since there was a *Germania* regiment already, and this was causing confusion, the title was changed to *Wiking*.

Where *Nordland* was concerned, Himmler had an enthusiastic acolyte. This was Vidkun Quisling who, before the war, had served as a minister in the

Above: Physical prowess was much emphasized in the *Waffen-SS*. Recruits had to be extremely fit, and events such as athletic trials were held to encourage both health and a sense of competition.

Norwegian Government and was a recipient of an honourary Commander of the Order of the British Empire. Subsequently, Quisling resigned to create the Norwegian Fascist Party and it was he who on 13 January 1941 appealed over the Norwegian radio for 3000 volunteers for the regiment. They would, he declared, be joining 'the war of freedom and independence against English world despotism'. The original upper age limit of 25 for recruitment was forthwith raised to 40, and Himmler lost no time in flying to Oslo to inspect the enthusiastic new recruits and officiate at

Right: The invasion of the Low Countries and France in the summer of 1940 provided further recruiting grounds for the *Waffen-SS*. The 'threat of Bolshevism' – in the form of the Soviet Union – helped swell their ranks.

their swearing in. After mustering, they were sent to Württemberg in southern Germany in order to train with the rest of the regiment in simulated battle conditions. Some of the new recruits were even able to experience the real thing; they were seconded to other SS units engaged in the Balkans.

Because of the urgent need to recruit more manpower for the war effort, the Nordic volunteers enjoyed less stringent service conditions than the Germans. This particularly galled Himmler with his goal of total loyalty from all his adherents, but pride had to be sacrificed in favour of sheer necessity. The Nordics were permitted to join on a 'hostilities only' basis, rather than the usual four-year term. Even the initial height restriction of 1.65m (5ft 5in) was waived and the oath of loyalty was modified in recognition of

the fact that the appeal among the volunteers was to nationalism rather than National Socialism, with the main aim being the destruction of Communism. But they received broadly the same pay and, with national distinctions, wore the same uniform as the regulars.

SINISTER DIRECTIVE

Elsewhere, Himmler was unstoppable. It had seemed to the *Reichsführer-SS* that the Dutch would be able to provide him with excellent racial material and in the summer of 1940 he had established the Regiment *Westland* which was to be open to volunteers from the Netherlands and Flanders. A recruiting initiative was launched with a leaflet entitled 'The *Waffen-SS* is Calling – You Too Should Protect Your Home Country'. It proclaimed:

'It would be absurd if you did not start fighting the enemy before he brutally demands entrance at the garden gate. This is not possible in a local war, and least possible at a time when continents are in revolt. Imagine a border landscape covered with snowdrifts and, breaking from the east, packs of ravening wolves which exterminate every kind of life.

'Does not this picture fit the present time as well?

'Who does not want to annihilate the ravening beasts who are breaking into the Fatherland? Do you mean simply to stand at the garden gate of your own home country? Then it will be too late. Happy the country that keeps the war far away from its boundaries and does not hesitate to make sacrifices in blood to save the fatherland.'

Rabble-rousing sentiment contrasted with other pronouncements infinitely more sinister. A directive was issued to all *Waffen-SS* members, the text of which survived to surface at the Nuremberg Trials: 'Obedience must be unconditional. It corresponds to the conviction that National Socialist ideology must reign supreme ... Every SS man is therefore prepared to carry out blindly every order issued by the Führer or given by his superior, regardless of the sacrifice involved.' Neither was the avowedly racist ethos of the

Below: Norwegian volunteers raise their right hands as they are sworn into the *Waffen-SS*. Although their helmets carry the SS runes, their collars do not yet have the SS insignia on them.

Above: *Reichsführer-SS* **Heinrich Himmler with Norway's wartime leader Vidkun Quisling, inspecting ranks of volunteers to the** *Waffen-SS* **who, at the outbreak of war, formed** *SS-Standarte Nordland* **within** *Wiking.*

armed SS in any way shirked. The SS was conceived as a Nazi aristocracy, as a new ruling class to create 'the New Order' which would consist of a National Socialist Military Order of Nordic Men, a fighting force '... bound by ideological oaths, whose fighters are selected from the best Aryan stock'. The predominant enemies were the Jews and the Bolsheviks.

The campaign worked. The *Reichsführer-SS* felt sufficiently encouraged by the enthusiastic response from volunteers to raise yet another regiment, *SS-Nordwest.* But Himmler tempered his enthusiasm with self-interested caution. Such volunteers, he declared, would remain firmly under central Nazi control, lest there be any hint of dissent in their ranks. Thus they were required to affirm the oath of loyalty to the *Waffen SS*: 'I swear to you Adolf Hitler, as leader, loyalty and courage. I pledge to you and to those you place in authority over me obedience even unto death. So help me God.' *Nordwest* as a regiment, it turned out, was to last until the German invasion of Russia, when it was deemed to have served its purpose. It survived in battalion form, with the bulk of its strength re-allocated to other Dutch or Flemish units of the *Waffen-SS.*

At first, there were noticeable gaps in the ranks once the first volunteers had been swallowed up. Then Reich Germans and ethnic Germans (*Volksdeutsche*) were drafted in. The result was that by the time of the invasion of the Soviet Union in 1941, *Wiking* contained 1142 Germanic volunteers: 630 Dutchmen, 294

Left: Among the most energetic of the Dutch recruits was Hendrik Feldmeijer, formerly a member of the bodyguard contingent to the puppet Netherlands premier Anton Mussert, whose members were required to join the SS.

Above: The *Westland* regiment had barely existed for three months before numbers swelled and a second battalion was formed. This propaganda photograph shows two Flemish soldiers reloading an MG 34.

Norwegians, 216 Danes, 1 Swede and 1 Swiss. In the same year would be added *Nordest*, a battalion consisting of Finns. Gottlob Berger worked hard in the cold land of Finland. Hatred and fear of Russia were played upon. Enquiries in pro-German Finnish circles revealed there were enough men in the country to form at least one *Waffen-SS* battalion. Subterfuge was necessary; the 1000 Finns who went to Germany did so as 'workers for the German war industry'.

The Finns were known to be a fiercely independent people; tactful treatment by Germany was therefore necessary. 'Guidelines for the behaviour of troops in Finland' was prepared. The document proclaimed:

'The Finn is a member of a cultured people, feeling strong associations to the other Scandinavian peoples, proud of his achievements and with a distinct sense of national pride. The freedom and independence of his country are valued above all. His friendliness towards Germans is genuine. ... anything that could hurt his national pride has to be avoided and his military achievement in particular has to be acknowledged.'

The Finnish reaction was lukewarm. The government made the stipulation that they would only fight Russians. The Army refused to take the *Waffen-SS* oath or be commanded by German officers. The upshot of the wrangling was that, by the start of 'Operation Barbarossa', 400 men were seconded to 5th *SS-Wiking*.

Thus were the endeavours of Himmler and Berger rewarded, but Hitler's preoccupations remained elsewhere, beyond even the impending campaign in the West. The invasion of the Soviet Union loomed ever nearer in the calculation of the supreme commander.

CHAPTER TWO

TRAINING

Waffen-SS volunteers were subjected to tough training, far harder than that of *Wehrmacht* recruits, with live ammunition regularly used in order to prepare the men for battle. *Wiking,* like the other *Waffen-SS* divisions, was also given priority over the *Wehrmacht* for the latest equipment.

When it came to training, the methods which applied to the Army differed considerably from those of the SS echelons. Thus many of the reforms instituted by Felix Steiner brought him into conflict with the rigid doctrines of Paul Hausser and the pre-World War II *Reichswehr* (Army). Along with so many of his generation, the battles of attrition that caused such heavy loss of life in World War I had haunted Steiner. It was his intention that the armed SS man would fight in very different conditions. Volunteers for this 'new race' were all undoubtedly wooed by the siren language of the recruiting leaflet:

'... The volunteer goes to Germany gladly, because he knows that the *Führer* keeps his word and that his family is being cared for in the best possible way.

... He will not be driven into battle as cannon fodder ... The blood of all the fighters of the *Führer* is too valuable to be risked at random. That is why the volunteer gets the best possible training in Germany which a soldier ever had, and the best weapons ever forged. The first pool of all volunteers from the other Germanic countries is the SS Training Camp at

Left: Men of the *Germania* Regiment enjoy a meal during their advance through France in the early summer of 1940. At this point the regiment was still part of the SS-VT Division, which would later become *Das Reich*.

Senneheim in Upper Alsace, where all those assemble who are brave and clever enough to make the leap into the future. The Germanic man does not have to be taught the hero ideal, it is burnt into his heart ... Enthusiastically, the militant mind will be in the forefront of battle for victory.'

COMPETITIVE SPIRIT

A noticeable innovation of the SS cadet schools was a shift in the priorities pertaining to the Army. Standards of education and a suitable background in politics no longer had major emphasis. This resulted, among other things, in some 40 per cent of the officer candidates accepted before 1938 having only elementary school education. This generated sharp criticism from the higher reaches of the Army. The professional quality of many pre-war SS officers compared unfavourably with their opposite numbers in the *Wehrmacht*.

On the positive side, there was Gottlob Berger's emphasis on strict military proficiency. The *Verfügungstruppen* as forerunner of the *Waffen-SS* may have had fewer numbers than the Army, but the physical calibre of its men was often higher. Exercise and sport became top of the agenda; there was everything from long- and short-distance running, to boxing, rowing, and a variety of track and field events. No longer would knots of men face their adversaries from the immobile fastness of trenches. Competitive spirit was created in sports and athletics, not in mock battles.

As far as practical army training went, the men of the SS learnt to become men on the move with assault troops, detachments and mobile battle groups. Differences in rank were less formal. *'Kamerad'* (comrade) was the accepted form of address and greeting, rather than adherence to rank and title. The regulation rifle was phased out in favour of weapons that were more mobile and easier to handle. This became the age of the submachine gun and the hand grenade. When it soon became apparent that, due to these innovations, it would be possible for troops not to be weighed down and to cover a distance of 3.2km (2 miles) in 20 minutes, even the most hidebound sections of the *Wehrmacht* were forced to take notice.

Below: Marksmanship, as demonstrated here by men of the *Totenkopf* Division in 1940, was a key part of training for the *Waffen-SS*. The rifleman uses sandbags to help steady his aim.

Early on, to be eligible for a commission in the SS-VT, there was a requirement for two years service in the ranks, which meant, in other words, in the pre-World War II *Reichswehr*. With the growth of the foreign SS legions and the exigencies of war, this stipulation was no longer possible, and faster programmes of training became essential. As was inevitable when a number of nationalities were involved, there were difficulties. One recruit to *Westland*, training in Munich, wrote:

'The language barrier first had to be overcome. So the Dutch comrades went to evening classes in German after a hard day's training. It was not difficult for the *Reich* Germans to carry out the hard basic training. As a rule they came from the Hitler Youth and had already been through pre-military instruction. In contrast the Dutch found the hard training particularly tough. In addition to the language problem, they had an aversion to 'Prussian drill' which was unknown in their homeland.'

In *European Volunteers*, an account of the wartime service of the 5th SS-Panzer-Division *Wiking*, Peter

Left: Even the toughest training programmes that could be devised for fledgling members of the *Waffen-SS* could only scarcely prepare them for the dangers and privations of the campaign in Russia.

Strassner, a former member of the division, states that the Danish volunteers who were engaged in training in Klagenfurt and in Vienna

'... were more robust and less sensitive than the Norwegians, loved good food and drink, but now and then were obstinate and tended to be strongly critical ... The Norwegians, on the other hand, worked harder and were more serious and contemplative. ... In their military achievements they developed an almost totally instinctive awareness which led them to be somewhat careless with regard to their own safety.'

Additionally, the intake from both nationalities had to cope with the prejudices of some instructors who considered that all foreigners were suitable only for barrack-room duties. However, many platoon and company commanders, and squad leaders, conscious that they were required to deliver potentially solid fighting material, knew they had to gain the cooperation of

Left: Even the toughest training programmes that could be devised for fledgling members of the *Waffen-SS* could only scarcely prepare them for the dangers and privations of the campaign in Russia.

those they were instructing. At the receiving end was Jan Munk, a recruit from *Westland* as part of the newly created *Wiking*, who underwent training at an *SS-Junkerschule*. He recalled:

'We liked the great majority of our superiors ... and not just liked them but respected them. If we were wet, cold and tired we knew that they would be as well. I only knew of one case of an NCO being disliked, a corporal, because of his treatment of the Flemish in particular. One Christmas night, when he was stoned out of his mind, we wrapped him in a blanket, dragged him feet first down the stairs to a cellar, threw him into one of the long washing troughs and turned on the cold water. He got a sound beating, and his colleagues turning a blind eye. He behaved much better afterwards.'

Another member of *Wiking* who had few complaints was the future *SS-Obersturmführer* Eric Brorup:

'I wasn't personally subjected to any form of demeaning or degrading treatment because I was a Dane. I went through officers' school where there was respect for every individual, not like the usual senseless bullshit you normally find – the US Military Academy at West Point. How hard was it? I can state quite categorically that the training I went through in the Danish Cavalry was tougher than anything I later encountered in the *Waffen-SS*. Manoeuvres were very realistic. With live ammunition being used on certain exercises, but not before every man knew his weapon and how to take cover ...'

That said, the training was certainly tough. At 05:00 hours came reveille, followed by washing, bed-making and mugs of coffee. Within the hour, the men were off to the training ground with their weapons. Manoeuvres were characterized by maximum realism, accompanied by heavy artillery barrages as well as live small-arms ammunition. Himmler learnt with great satisfaction that his men thought little of being 100m (300ft) from explosions from their own artillery fire.

A midday break, not for rest but weapon-cleaning and boot-polishing, was followed by continued training until 17:00 hours. This was followed by yet more cleaning and polishing. The pleasure of dinner was blunted by the knowledge that classroom lectures in combat would follow until the close of the day's work, which came finally at 22:00 hours.

HARD DISCIPLINE

Hard discipline sometimes meant humiliation for the recruit at the hands of a martinet instructor. If a recruit, while filling cartridges into a charger, let a cartridge fall to the ground, he could be made to pick it up with his teeth. One recruit who let a cartridge slip in this way and attempted to rescue it by hand described the reaction of an NCO:

'... He went scarlet, bellowed out something unintelligible, handed the section over to his deputy and took me on himself. He began with 50 "knee bends" with rifle held out at arms length ... After 20 knee bends I stopped counting. I just couldn't go on. I did one more knee bend and then I lowered my rifle and stood up. I just knew I was all in. I heard him bellowing and that left me cold because suddenly I could control myself no longer. I felt I had to weep although I knew it was neither manly nor soldierly. I had just had enough. When he saw that, he bellowed: "Look at this! Mollycoddle! Mother's little darling! Cry baby! Who's ever heard of an SS man blubbering! All our dead will turn in their graves! Is this what we're trying to take to war" etc etc. Then "assembly" was blown and the training period ended. He ordered me to clean out all the first floor latrines for a week and then report to him so that he could inspect them. And straightaway he ordered: "Chuck this cartridge away." I did so. I picked it up with my teeth.'

The toughness of these training programmes intensified. Even when it came to going on leave, a recruit would be required to have his handkerchief folded with the required number of creases. If a pay-book produced an unsightly bulge in a uniform the offender ran the risk of being deprived of his pay. Matters became even more stringent in the shadow of war when the aim was to complete basic training by

Above: This photograph of a *Wiking* Division *Hauptscharführer* (Warrant Officer) was taken in Russia on 10 January 1944. Note his *Germania* cuff title and infantry assault and wound badges.

September 1940. At that time the men were informed by a '*Führer* order' that a new division would be formed. The composition of the motorized *SS-Wiking* Division was drawn from the three infantry regiments, *Germania*, *Westland*, and *Nordland*, together with an artillery regiment and a signals and pioneer battalion, as well as further divisional troops.

Some idea of the relative speed of this achievement can be gained when it is recalled that, at the beginning of World War II, only the *Leibstandarte* Division was a motorized formation, whereas the SS-VT and *Totenkopf* regiments were basic infantry formations and as such employed transport which was predominantly drawn by the age-old method of using horses.

INSIGNIA AND UNIFORM

The men of the regiments which made up *SS-Panzer-Division Wiking* or who fought with the division were especially keen to retain their national identity and sense of pride. Himmler had, therefore, at first been in favour of limiting the wearing of SS rank badges to SS members rather than co-opted volunteers, but the implication that non-SS members were regarded as somehow inferior caused offence and therefore led to the idea being abandoned.

The matter of collar patches remains a source of confusion among historians and insignia specialists. Some sources maintain that the SS-runes were worn on the right side of the collar throughout the existence of *Wiking*, while others state that a badge comprising the prow of a Viking ship *(Schiffssteven)* was proposed. In September 1942, the division was awarded a cuff-title bearing the word *'Wiking'*. For officers, the *Wiking* lettering was machine-woven in aluminium wire and black silk thread edged with white silk thread. The gothic version was seemingly exclusive to *SS-Obergruppenführer und General der Waffen-SS* (General) Herbert Gille, who in May 1943 became the divisional commander of *Wiking*.

Other ranks displayed a cuff-band with a machine-embroidered inscription in silver-grey silk thread and grey silk edging. There was also a cuff-band for all ranks that was machine-woven in silver-grey and black silk thread. Cuffs displaying regimental titles for *Germania*, *Nordland* and *Westland* – styled in standard lettering – remained. As far as *Westland* was concerned, a source of confusion were two particularly striking shoulder straps introduced in May 1940. These carried the initial 'W', often confused with *Wiking* itself. The importance attached to symbolism in SS regalia was another manifestation of Himmler's preoccupation with what he saw as the romantic trappings of Germany's past. The distinguished British historian John Keegan has since commented:

'Himmler's resort to the use of individual titles and to the emphasis on unit identities was, in the national context, an extremely clever psychological stroke by a man striving to build up a large military force solely through the medium of voluntary enlistment. For the

Above: The *SS-Freiwilligen-Legion Norwegen*, to which this man belonged, was the first Norwegian SS unit to be formed. By March 1942 it could muster 1200 men, but a grim future awaited it in a matter of months.

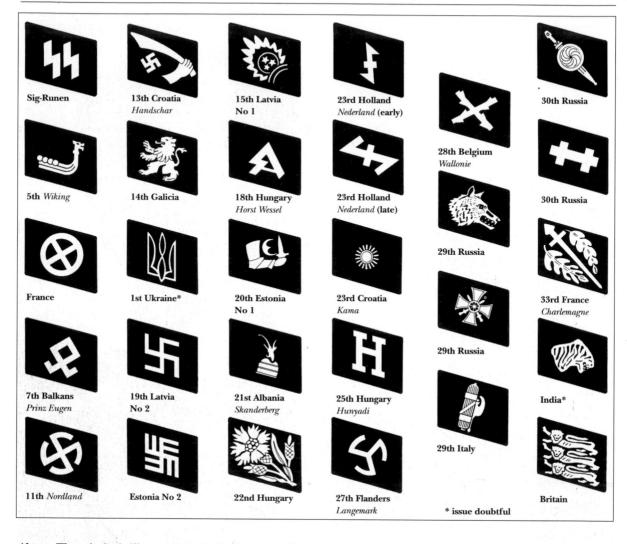

Sig-Runen

13th Croatia
Handschar

15th Latvia
No 1

23rd Holland
Nederland (early)

30th Russia

5th *Wiking*

14th Galicia

18th Hungary
Horst Wessel

23rd Holland
Nederland (late)

28th Belgium
Wallonie

30th Russia

France

1st Ukraine*

20th Estonia
No 1

23rd Croatia
Kama

29th Russia

33rd France
Charlemagne

7th Balkans
Prinz Eugen

19th Latvia
No 2

21st Albania
Skanderberg

25th Hungary
Hunyadi

29th Russia

India*

11th *Nordland*

Estonia No 2

22nd Hungary

27th Flanders
Langemark

29th Italy

Britain

* issue doubtful

Above: These insignia illustrate graphically the eventually rapid expanse of *Waffen-SS* manpower from outside the *Reich*. The various countries shown were encouraged to use national or regional symbols.

Right: *Wiking* officers at the beginning of 'Operation Barbarossa' in Russia, 1941. The man in the foreground is an *SS-Obersturmführer* (First Lieutenant), while on his right is an *SS-Untersturmführer* (Second Lieutenant).

old Kaiser's army had been built on the principle of strong unit identity and on a hierarchy of regiments, with the Guards at the top. Hitler had deliberately reconstructed the *Wehrmacht* on a pattern which owed nothing to the past and made no differentiation between one unit and another, since he wanted the new army to be entirely his own. In fulfilling that wish, however, he undoubtedly frustrated a strongly-

established element in the German attitude to military service. Himmler, by recognizing the German soldier's inclination to belong to an identifiable and élite formation ... attracted many who would not otherwise have been drawn to so politically tainted an organization.'

The deep-seated longing to revive the ethos of Germany's military past was symbolized by Himmler for the SS in the device of the *Totenkopf*, a grim motif

made up of a skull and crossed bones. With such a lineage, Himmler eagerly sought the Death's Head for his SS. It was the only badge common to all SS formations, whether *Allgemeine-SS, Germanic-SS,* or *Waffen-SS*; the latter comprised German and non-German formations. The *Totenkopf* harked back to the 18th century heyday of Prussian cavalry regiments when it formed the centrepiece of the cap of the 'Black' or 'Death' Hussars, while the headpiece of the 9th Hussars – known as the 'Total Death' Hussars – sported a reclining skeleton. In World War I, the *Totenkopf* device served as a formation badge for a number of crack German units and in the days of the Weimar Republic was sported on the helmets and vehicles belonging to the 'freebooting' and notorious *Freikorps.*

Another *Wiking* symbol was the so-called 'Sun-cross' or round swastika *(Sonnerad)* which, while being *Wiking's* divisional badge, was also adopted by the *Germanische SS-Panzer-Korps.* Usually occupying a prominent position on tanks, it could be mounted either upright or in the 'mobile' position. The Sun-cross also served as the cuff-band in block lettering for members of *SS-Infanterie-Regiment Nordland.*

Lavish Promises

Norwegians also made up the strength of SS-*Freiwilligen* (Volunteer) *Legion Norske,* many of whom were later to merge with *Wiking* to form 11th *SS-Freiwilligen-Panzergrenadier Nordland.* This legion was officially launched at a massive recruiting rally staged on University Square in Oslo, following the invasion of Russia in June 1941. The Norwegian Post Office issued a stamp with a suitably idealistic design, showing a soldier leading comrades into battle in his Norwegian uniform, flanked by Norwegian and Finnish flags. The Germans made lavish promises to all the Germanic legions: their national identities and military traditions would be respected. But the Nazis were not over-scrupulous in honouring this. In the case of the *Legion Norske,* the men were told that they would not be allowed to wear Norwegian Army uniforms with French-style helmets, but were expected to wear the standard *Waffen-SS* field-grey uniforms. However, a standard legion collar patch, worn on the right and

Above: The *Waffen-SS,* in common with much of the *Wehrmacht,* was keen on recording much of its early successes on film for propaganda purposes. The cameraman is attached to the *SS-Standarte Nordland.*

displaying a rampant axe-bearing Norwegian lion, was permitted. *Waffen-SS* rank insignia was worn on the left collar patch and on shoulder straps.

For those who relished the prospect of front-line fighting and of proving their undoubted valour, it was announced that there would be an imposing medal: the St Olaf's Cross with crossed swords and the date 1941 in the centre. But although the design was generally approved within Norway, the German authorities declined to sanction it. The medal was not issued. By way of consolation, all Norwegians who served on the

Eastern Front – including, incidentally, a sizeable number of nurses – received a special 'Frontiers' badge in silver or white metal. The badge depicted a medieval Norwegian warrior grasping a shield and drawn sword and standing in an archway bearing the lettering *'Frontkjemper'* (Frontfighter) in pseudo-runic script. On 1 August 1941, Himmler ordered that the full name of the Volunteer Legion was to be worn on cuff bands.

Former members of '*Hird*', the group of 'Storm Troopers' founded by the arch-collaborationist Vidkun Quisling, were permitted to wear the *Hird* emblem on their left cuff above the Legion band. As a further tribute, the 1st Battalion would receive the name *Viken* in honour of the No 1 *Hird* Regiment. Four infantry companies made up the 1st Battalion, with an antitank company and a war correspondents' section. Later, a

Below: Norwegian volunteers disembarking at a German port. Ahead of these keen, fresh-faced young men lie many weeks of vigorous training for combat. Norwegians gained a reputation for being hard, relentless fighters.

2nd (Reserve) Battalion was established and it was quartered at Holmestrand, outside Oslo.

On the eve of their departure for Poland, the first 800 volunteers from Belgium, who left Brussels on 8 August 1941 and who formed the nucleus of the recently raised *Legion Wallonien*, marched behind a Colour Party bearing the Legion's first flag. Their flag featured a stylized version of the Red Ragged Cross of Burgundy on a field of black. The colour black was intended as a tribute to the Rexist Party and its founder Leon Degrelle. This device lasted until the following March, when new colours and guidons were introduced to replace the black Rexist flag. When the Legion went on active service, the colours went too.

As for the stubborn Finns, they insisted on sticking to their own volunteer battalion name, *Finnisches Freiwilligen Bataillon der Waffen-SS* and kept their own banner in the form of the blue cross flag of Finland. This incorporated, among other motifs, the national emblem of a gold lion and swords, together with the commemorative cross of the 27th *Jägerbataillon* of

World War I. The original Finnish SS-Volunteer Battalion *Nordost* had been sent in June 1941 to provide muscle for 5th SS Division *Wiking* in the campaign against the Soviet Union. Its name was subsequently changed to *Finnisches Freiwilligen Bataillon der Waffen-SS* (Finnish Volunteer Battalion of the *Waffen-SS*). It was then presented with a highly distinctive colour, consisting of the square flag of Finland, a broad light blue cross on a white field. In a simplified version of the Finnish coat of arms, the Golden Lion of Finland was featured on the square, rampant and also brandishing a silver sword facing the staff and trampling upon the silver scimitar of Russia, Finland's sworn enemy. The colour was bordered on three sides with a fringe of strands which were gold-coloured.

WEAPONS

As Bruce Quarrie points out in *Weapons of the Waffen-SS* – which examines in detail the development and tactical use of the vast range of weaponry employed by the *Waffen-SS* – one of the greatest sources of dispute remains the assertion that *Waffen-SS* units were favoured when it came to the allotment of weapons. The Army was then made to suffer in consequence. But a substantial number of *Waffen-SS* men have alleged the contrary, even admitting that under the cover of darkness, raiding parties were organized in order to steal weapons from Army stores.

Himmler's legions had at first to put up with captured Czech weapons that were unfamiliar. Even in 1940, in the face of an escalating war, the Army declined to surrender any heavy artillery to the SS until Hitler personally intervened. Two years later, armaments minister Albert Speer was persuaded to allocate five to eight per cent of his factories' output to the *Waffen-SS* with manpower for the task provided by concentration camp inmates. One of the reasons for this slow provision of armaments can be attributed to the attitude of superiority adopted by the *Wehrmacht* who

Right: The Norwegian fascist leader Vidkun Quisling is seen here with *SS-Reichsführer* Heinrich Himmler visiting *Wiking* divisional staff in 1941 on the Russian Front. Quisling was tried for treason and executed in late 1945.

regarded the *Waffen-SS* as 'asphalt soldiers' obsessed with parade-ground drill and spit and polish. 'Policemen dressed up in army uniforms' was the sneering judgement of General Walther von Brauchitsch, who was commander-in-chief of the *Wehrmacht* during the Polish campaign.

But as the war progressed, it became widely recognized that the *Waffen-SS* forces had become at least the equal of the *Wehrmacht* units and certainly superior in ferocity and fanaticism. This points to the reason why, by November 1942, the four heavily battle-scarred *Waffen-SS* divisions – *Leibstandarte Adolf Hitler, Das Reich, Totenkopf,* and *Wiking* – had all been withdrawn to be refitted with a strong tank component, together with assault guns and armoured personnel carriers. To underline the point, they were officially designated *SS-Panzergrenadier* divisions and, furthermore, had the benefit of equipment of a quality comparable to that of the Army panzer divisions.

SUPPORT WEAPONS

At the opening of 'Operation Barbarossa', the invasion of the Soviet Union in June 1941, the three regiments of volunteers, under the umbrella of *Wiking*, served initially with the *Leibstandarte*, now at brigade strength, as part of Army Group South. In terms of hardware, *Wiking's* partner could call on the 1st, 2nd and 3rd Battalions, each of three rifle companies, one machine-gun company and one heavy company. The heavy company had two antitank-gun platoons (3.7cm/1.46in PaK and 5cm/1.97in PaK), one platoon of mortars (8cm/3.15in), and one pioneer platoon. In addition, there was the 4th Heavy Battalion, which consisted of one light infantry-gun company (7.5cm/2.95in guns), one heavy infantry-gun company (15cm/5.9in guns), one antitank gun company (4.7cm/1.85in self-propelled PaK), one field-gun company (7.5cm/2.95in self-propelled guns), and one anti-aircraft-gun company (3.7cm/1.46in AA guns).

Left: The 7.92mm (3.1in) MG 34 machine gun is seen here as an antiaircraft weapon and on vehicle mounts. Even with an astounding rate of fire, the MG34 was seen as a liability: it took too long to manufacture.

In the field, the *Wehrmacht* and the *Waffen-SS* divisions and regiments could call on the finest individual infantry support weapons, most notably machine guns (*Maschinegewehr*), including the MG 34, rated by many to be the finest machine gun of the war. When it came to small arms, the pistol, although of limited value in combat, had its place as a small weapon which could be carried conveniently by the crews of tanks and other armoured fighting vehicles. Norwegian volunteers in *Wiking* made plentiful use of the home-grown Model 1914 11.43mm (0.45in) automatic pistol, a licence-built copy of the famous Colt pistol.

FINNISH MASTERPIECE

A valuable role was also filled by Finnish forces who had good reason to loathe the Russians since, after a fiercely fought 15-week war with them in November 1939, Finland had been forced to cede some 41,430 square kilometres (16,000 square miles) of territory. In their fight on the side of Germany as the 3rd Battalion of *Nordland*, the Finns strengthened the submachine gun (SMG) stocks within the *Waffen-SS*. The ingeniously crafted Suomi M/1931 had proved itself in the earlier conflict against the Russians. It was reliable and well-fashioned: all metal parts were machine-made and jamming was virtually unknown.

The provision of tanks and armoured fighting vehicles for the crack SS divisions received a boost in February 1943. This month saw the return to active

Below: *Waffen-SS* troopers on the Eastern Front in 1941, with their weapons ready to hand. All wear the camouflage smock patented by the *Waffen-SS*, which legally prevented the *Wehrmacht* from using camouflage uniforms.

duty of General Heinz Guderian as Inspector General of Armoured Troops. Previously, Guderian had been sacked by Hitler. His mistake was daring to disagree with the *Führer* over the conduct of the war. But he was restored to favour after serious military setbacks for the Germans, and after that point he was entrusted with implementing every aspect of recruitment, training, organization, and equipment for the panzer divisions, including that of the *Waffen-SS*.

With their elevation to the status of *Panzergrenadier* divisions for the spring counteroffensive in Russia, *Leibstandarte* Adolf Hitler, *Das Reich, Totenkopf,* and *Wiking* were each backed by a tank battalion. Assault weapons had previously been assigned to artillery rather than panzer formations. This turned out to be a miscalculation that Guderian would soon remedy.

At the end of 1943, control of assault weapons passed to the panzer arm, to be seized with enthusiasm by *Hohenstaufen* and *Frundsberg,* both of which had been elevated to *Panzergrenadier* division status, and later by *Hitler*

Above: On the left of the picture is an SdKfz armoured car, and on the right a PzKpfw III, both on the Eastern Front, the latter, in the early stages of the war, regarded as among the best of the all-round medium tanks.

Jugend. Included also in control of the weapons were to be seven other panzer and *Panzergrenadier* formations, including *Nordland* and *Wallonien.*

At the time of the outbreak of World War II, the PzKpfw IV, known as Panzer IV – *Panzerkampfwagen* means armoured fighting vehicle – was considered to be among the best of the all-round medium tanks, and was employed by *Wiking* on the Eastern Front during the winter of 1941–42. Indeed, it would survive until the end of the war. Later in 1942 on the Eastern Front the PzKpfw IV Ausf G (*Ausführung* G: 'Model G') appeared. But as was the case with these, and so many of the tank arm, the true enemy was the unrelenting sub-zero temperatures of the Russian winters which, in the end, no matter how powerful they were, would eventually defeat them.

CHAPTER THREE

BLOODED

In the early days of 'Barbarossa', German successes came with relative ease. Russian forces were unprepared, but it soon became apparent that they had a big advantage in armour. The men of *Wiking* were bolstered by the claim that 'the gateway to the Caucasus had been opened'.

The summons of the senior military commanders to a conference in Hitler's mountain retreat in the Obersalzberg on 29 August 1939 followed a predictable course. The substance of long-winded dissertation was that Foreign Minister Joachim Ribbentrop had been sent to Moscow to sign a non-aggression pact that would lead to the carve-up of Poland in just four days. A new eastern frontier could be created to serve as a protectorate state, acting, if necessary, as a buffer against Russia. Regarding a role for the *Waffen-SS*, Hitler was vague. But one hint was sinister enough; it was made clear that Himmler's men were expected to carry out 'special tasks' which, ominously, 'would not be to the taste of German generals'.

The outlook had never been anything but dire for Poland. The material which the Polish commanders had at their disposal was mostly slow-moving infantry. Alongside 30 infantry divisions there were only 2 motorized brigades and 11 cavalry brigades. The most armour that could be mustered was nine companies of 8128kg (8-ton) tanks and 29 companies of armoured weapon carriers. Some 92 per cent of Poland's military

Left: In this pre-war photo, Adolf Hitler is seen in characteristic pose at a gathering of senior SS and *Wehrmacht* officers. On the left is Paul Hausser, inspector of the *Verfügungstruppen* and Commander of *Das Reich*.

wheeled transport was horse-drawn. This is not to say that the overall strength of the *Waffen-SS* was over impressive. At this stage, *Leibstandarte* Adolf Hitler was only a regiment, the sole one to be motorized among the *Waffen-SS* units. The German Army depended on horses for more than 80 per cent of its motive power.

CASE WHITE

Hitler's intention was that armoured formations would unleash a series of surprise attacks. These were Army Group South, made up of the Seventh, Tenth and Fourteenth Armies under the overall control of General Gerd von Rundstedt, and Army Group North whose components were Third and Fourth Armies under General Fedor von Bock. There was to be a pincer envelopment by the two army groups. The jaws of the pincer would clamp against the six Polish armies which were deployed in a defensive cordon along the line of the Vistula River. Bock's group would converge on the Polish corridor from both sides, East Prussia and Pomerania. The link-up in the corridor would be followed by a westward advance towards Warsaw. The Tenth Army, under General Walther von Reichenau received *SS-Leibstandarte* and the *SS-Pioniersturmbann*. SS-Regiment *Germania*, a future component of *Wiking*, was part of Fourteenth Army, under General Wilhelm List, and was held at first in reserve in East Prussia.

On 30 August, the German High Command sent out the codewords setting the action day of *Fall Weiss* (Case White) as 1 September and H-hour as 04:45 hours. For those commanders who itched impatiently for the word of command, the open and rolling terrain proved ideal for the strike force of 55 divisions, including every armoured, motorized and light division the *Reich* possessed. The reserve status of *Germania* was short lived. Soon it was entrusted with protecting the weak flank of XXII Army Corps in the drive towards Chelm as part of Tenth Army which had gone into the attack from Silesia. There were also gaps in the lines of VIII Army Corps, 5th Panzer Division and the Army Reconnaissance Unit. It was *Germania*'s task, under the command of *SS-Standartenführer* (Colonel) Carl-Maria Demelhuber, to fill them.

TOWARDS WARSAW

In the advance through the industrial region towards Lvov, the SS encountered stiff resistance and high casualties. The Poles were the butt of incessant air- and ground attacks. With their supplies and ammunition annihilated, the Poles capitulated around the area of Blonie and the *Leibstandarte* was able to continue its advance towards Warsaw. The capital, in the face of starvation and typhoid, managed to hold out, but had to give up finally on 27 September.

The experience of *Germania* in Poland, although nothing in comparison with what was to come, had been of value, providing the fledgling products of the SS training schools the chance to hear their first shots fired in anger. In addition, Poland provided another pointer to the future: those in command of the SS-VT declared that they had been badly in need of strong support at *Wehrmacht* divisional level which had been denied them. It was a grumble that was to become increasingly familiar from the time that the *Wiking* Division, whose creation was announced by Hitler on 21 December 1940, went into action.

Right: Resistance was largely overcome with ease during the 1939 attack on Poland. Although bombed and shelled, the town of Sochaczew put up one of the strongest defences against the *Waffen-SS*.

Above: These *Waffen-SS* soldiers in Poland are part of a reconnaissance team seen at the start of the campaign in September 1939. The SS sometimes encountered fierce resistance and suffered high casualties.

Felix Steiner had been given command of the *Wiking* Division and its divisional appointed regiments. Five days later, he visited *Germania* in order to give lectures down to company level. He was speaking on the potential of heavy infantry weapons, as well as issuing more general instruction on tactics. Then theory had soon given way to practice, with instructional courses for the NCOs of the heavy- and light machine-gun companies. Furthermore, training for the entire Division had continued throughout the iron winter of 1941. A member of 10th Panzergrenadier Regiment *Westland* wrote at the time:

'We have got deep snow here and it is terribly cold. And everyday we do one hour's sport in the open only in track suits. That really is cold. Last week, I had a severe cold for a few days, but now I am completely fit again, without having to report sick for a single day. We can hardly allow ourselves to be ill at this moment. We now know with fair certainty that we are no longer very far from going into action on the front. In the last four days we have not even had time to think. We have had to work hard until late in the night. We had an examination on Friday and Saturday and such a one as I have never experienced.'

On the eve of 'Operation Barbarossa', the intended role for the non-German volunteers was highlighted by the Nazi-controlled media. One newspaper proclaimed:

'Aryan man is realizing already during this war the new concept of a just order of society and a fruitful cooperation. Fighting shoulder to shoulder against the Bolsheviks alongside the Germans are Finns, Norwegians, Danes, Dutchmen, Frenchman, Spaniards, Croats, Italians, Hungarians, Romanians, Slovaks, Swedes, Flemings, Walloons – in short the whole of Europe. The stream of volunteers is endless.'

MORALE BOOSTER

For the benefit of home consumption, the Propaganda Ministry of Josef Goebbels was whipping up support for the *Waffen-SS*. A typical morale booster was a radio feature called *The SS at War*, broadcast in part from a recruitment centre. A transcript of one survived:

'The men, tall and fair, are standing here in a long file; these men have volunteered for service in some division of the *Waffen-SS*, in the *Leibstandarte*, the *Das Reich* Division, the *Wiking* Division, or the *Totenkopf* Division. Every SS man who does his duty in the

homeland today has been, or will be again within a short time, a soldier in the ranks of the *Waffen-SS* or the armed forces, and he performs his duty as a soldier in the knowledge that if he is killed on active service the great SS community of comrades in the homeland will stand by his dependents and will give them more than financial security. The welfare department of the *Waffen-SS* and the comrades in the units of the SS vie with each other in their care for the dependents of their dead.'

On the night of 19/20 June, a mass of German armour, headlights masked into narrow beams, edged into the central Polish forest of Pratulin, a few miles

Below: Atrocities, both in Poland and Russia, were carried out by the *Waffen-SS*, a number of which were laid at the door of *SS-Wiking*, including the killing of 600 Galician Jews 'as a reprisal for Soviet cruelties'.

short of the Bug river, an area which was the central sector of occupied Poland, the German frontier with the Soviet Union. In terms of numbers, there were in all more than 3 million men, 600,000 vehicles and 3350 tanks, spread along a 2000km (1250 mile) front stretching from the Baltic to the Black Sea, and constituting the greatest military machine ever assembled to make war. The leading panzer corps flexed their muscles for the planned assault on the River Bug while *Germania* was tasked with clearing the wooded country for the planned advance. This was followed by a blooding for the men of the 5th Artillery Regiment of *Nordland*, one of whose batteries, with its reconnaissance units and antitank weaponry, was making over rising terrain towards Tarnopol in Galicia at a time when the Russian defences were still insufficient to stop the *Waffen-SS* advance.

Above: Foreign *Waffen-SS* volunteers man a PaK antitank gun during the early stages of Operation 'Barbarossa'. Although the Red Army had some advanced T-34 tanks, the majority faced by the *Waffen-SS* were obsolescent.

Through his binoculars, the battery's commander spotted a mass of Russian tanks on the move with assorted camouflaged personnel carriers and motor cycles. The battery's firepower first caught a stationery carrier whose crew ran for their lives, then the battery turned its full fury on the tanks. The extent to which reinforcements contributed to the final success of the overall assault could not be determined exactly. In his *European Volunteers*, Peter Strasser records: 'A total of 48 tanks and 100 other combat vehicles were later counted on the battlefield. The danger to the division's left flank had been removed, and the advance towards Tarnopol could resume.'

At Tarnopol itself the SS volunteer forces became associated for the first time with the darker side of the *Waffen-SS,* embodied in the sinister *Einsatzgruppen* (extermination squads) which had been created by Himmler. These squads were to follow the German armies into the Soviet Union to combat resistance groups and to execute 'political and racial undesirables'. Combat groups were posted to the *Einsatzgruppen* as 'a recognized part of *Waffen-SS* discipline'. An *Einsatzgruppen* report of 11 July stated that '600 Jews were executed at Zborow between Tarnopol and Lwow [Lvov] by the *Waffen SS* as a reprisal for Soviet cruelties.' *Wiking* forces had been present at the time, along with the Divisional supply contingent *(Verwaltungsamt)* under *Wiking's* Supply Officer Heinz Karl Fanslau, who had been Paul Hausser's adjutant at Bad Tolz. During the course of war-crimes trials held at Nuremberg during August 1947, Fanslau testified that the supply battalion had arrived at a crossroads outside Tarnopol at a time when the Germans were bombing. They were 300–500m (980–1640ft) south of the road on which the main column of the Division was advancing. It was alleged that Fanslau had witnessed an *Oberscharführer* (Staff Sergeant) Saan taking away three Jews for execution and that Fanslau had told a small boy, who was accompanying his father, to stop crying or he would be shot as well. It was also attested at the trial that when *Standartenführer* (Colonel) Hilmar Wackerle, the regimental commander of *SS-Westland,* was shot dead, an order had been issued by Fanslau stating that the Jews were responsible and that from now on killing them would no longer be a punishable offence.

MASSACRES

It was around this time that the *Einsatzgruppen* massacres took place. An order had also been given at Tarnopol that Jews were to be assembled for work and if it was later discovered that they were ill suited, they were to be transported to ghettos. Oswald Pohl, one of the accused, testified that the supply company of *Wiking* employed Jews and ill-treated them. As divisional supply officer, Fanslau was acquitted of having a

connection with the massacre order. Fate eventually caught up with him; re-arrested on other charges, he was tried and sentenced to 25 years imprisonment. In later years, surviving members of *Wiking* have claimed that their men spent the war purely and solely as combat troops, but even so, they have been unable to escape a sinister association with the *Einsatzgruppen* one of whose formations, *Einsatzgruppe* A, was active in the northern sector of the Russian Front in the same year as the events in Tarnopol. It included 340 members of the *Waffen-SS* in a complement of 990. Nor were all the men of *Wiking* innocent of direct involvement in atrocities. Peter Neumann, a ticket collector's son from

Above: Fraternization between the people of Ukraine and the men of *Wiking* was common enough in the early days of 'Barbarossa'; the German forces were initially welcomed as liberators from Moscow's rule.

Wittenburg who had been a member of the Hitler Youth before joining *Wiking* as a junior officer, witnessed the treatment meted out by a fellow *Obersturmführer* (First Lieutenant) to unsuspecting captured Russian civilians, particularly if they sported a tell-tale gold star on the sleeve. The *Obersturmführer* would ask: 'You are a People's Commissar?' ('*Narodnii Kommissar li vou?*'). Invariably caught off guard by the casual tone of the question, the prisoner would nod. This was a prelude to a bullet to the head. The net was cast wider. In the area of Zhitomir, *Wiking* celebrated its success by reducing the town to ruins. Instructions were given to search every ruined home and building for, in addition to People's Commissars, all of the town's officials whether civilian or military. Once rounded up, they were shot. An SS report survived to be placed in evidence at the Nuremberg Trials:

'In the neighbourhood north of Zhitomir 12 villages were screened and a total of 15 functionaries liquidated. In the course of an investigation of the village of Techernjachov and in search for Communist functionaries, 31 Jews who were active Communists and also acted partly as political commissars were executed.'

EXECUTIONS

'In the course of an action carried out in Rudjina and Trojanov, 26 Jewish Communists and saboteurs were seized and shot. In the centre of the big square a gallows was erected for two Jewish murderers who were hanged there. Around the place of execution was a crowd of several thousand people. The *Wehrmacht* was also represented in large numbers. In addition, 400 Jews were made to witness the execution. Before the execution took place, the loudspeaker van announced in German and Ukrainian the deeds of horror committed by the two men, Keiper and his assistant, and the proposed penalty. In addition, two big posters which were fixed on the gallows, indicated once more the crime committed. The pronouncing of the sen-

Left: Prepared roads in Russia were virtually non-existent. Major routes were nothing more than mud tracks which were extremely dusty in summer, almost impassable in spring and autumn, and rutted and rock-hard in winter.

Right: The Russian frontier, which is indicated by the striped column on the right of the picture, is crossed by *Waffen-SS* motorcyclists of a reconaissance battalion coming from the German-occupied Polish territory.

tence was repeatedly interrupted by calls of approval and applause. The indigenous population accepted, with particularly great satisfaction, this measure of retaliation for Jewish horrors committed over a period of 10 years.

Afterwards 402 Jews from Zhitomir were shot. The execution of two Jewish murderers as well as the shooting of the 402 Jews was carried out in an exemplary manner. In Radomyschl the newly appointed mayor was unmasked as an informer of the NKVD and a member of the Communist Party since 1925. It was also proved that up to the last day he was in touch with Communist bands. His deputy was also a Bolshevik ... Jews were also arrested who openly had opposed the German forces and had refused to work for the labour organization. In this action, 113 persons were shot.'

SWITCH TO UMAN

Fresh for action, the 3rd Company of the Regiment *Westland* started its war by making for Lemberg and beyond in blazing sunshine where the Soviet 32nd Infantry Division had amassed. Here *Westland's* Dutch, Finnish and German forces disposed of a Russian attack with light and heavy machine guns, 8cm (3.15in) mortars and rifles. Reserves of ammunition reached the firing positions in sufficient strength to ensure the weakening of the Soviet attack, which was finally beaten off by the regiment's reconnaissance battalion with fast scout cars and motorcycle infantry. In the face of such puny opposition, the remark of a *Wehrmacht* lieutenant, for all its arrogance, could perhaps be understood: 'The Russian defences might have been a row of glass-houses.'

The crossing of the steeply banked River Slutsch (or Slucz), that ran south of Minsk, near the small village of Husyantin, was in response to reconnaissance reports of movement by enemy columns and goods trains. The 1st Battalion of *Haupsturmführer* (Captain) Hajo von Hadeln seized the crossing in a surprise night

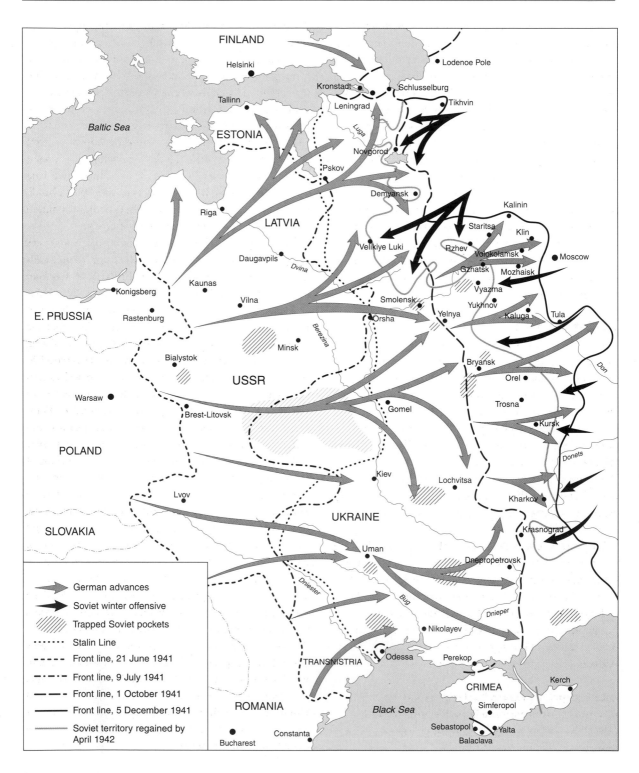

FINLAND

Helsinki

Lodenoe Pole

Kronstadt
Schlusselburg
Tikhvin
Leningrad

Tallinn

ESTONIA

Baltic Sea

Luga

Novgorod

Pskov

LATVIA

Demyansk

Riga

Kalinin

Velikiye Luki
Staritsa
Klin

Daugavpils

Dvina

Rzhev
Volokolamsk

Kaunas

Gzhatsk
Mozhaisk
Moscow

Vilna

Smolensk
Yelnya
Vyazma

Konigsberg

Orsha
Yukhnov

E. PRUSSIA
Rastenburg

Kaluga
Tula

Berezina

Minsk

Bryansk

Bialystok

Orel
Don

USSR

Warsaw

Trosna

Brest-Litovsk

Gomel

Kursk

Kiev

Lochvitsa

Donets

POLAND

Lvov

Kharkov

SLOVAKIA

UKRAINE

Krasnograd

Uman

Dnepropetrovsk

German advances

Dniester

Bug

Soviet winter offensive

Dnieper

Trapped Soviet pockets

Nikolayev

Stalin Line

TRANSNISTRIA
Odessa
Perekop

Front line, 21 June 1941

Front line, 9 July 1941

Kerch

Front line, 1 October 1941

CRIMEA

Front line, 5 December 1941

ROMANIA
Simferopol

Soviet territory regained by
April 1942

Black Sea

Sebastopol
Yalta

Bucharest
Constanta
Balaclava

attack, followed by a lightning advance to the village outskirts. The Russians, unleashing their firepower, prepared to regain the bridge. *Westland* returned the onslaught with interest. Exceptional bravery was demonstrated by six men of 17th Company under *Oberjunker* Vogel. These three Germans, two Dutchmen and one Dane, returning from a reconnaissance, joined in the fray and perished. All of that Sunday in July the Russians kept up the pressure until the newly arrived 1st Mountain Division of the *Wehrmacht* came to relieve the beleaguered SS. At this time, a combat report by 1st Company pinpointed a crucial weakness in the Germans that was to become all too familiar: scant knowledge of the fighting terrain. Amid the tall corn and maize fields, Russian snipers could hide themselves effectively, and their accurate fire inflicted heavy losses on the Germans.

TORRENTIAL RAIN

The relief of *Westland* was followed by a change of weather with sunshine giving way to a torrential downpour that reduced roads to morasses of mud and slowed any effective advance. When movement was again possible there was a push eastwards on foot for four days through heavily wooded terrain. The divisional history – *Panzer Grenadiere der Panzer Division Wiking* – recorded the discovery of 'a great mass of abandoned Russian equipment, bridled horses and petrol stores which the Soviet had not been able to evacuate. It showed clearly that the enemy had retreated in disorder.'

Elsewhere on the Slutsch near Satanov, the fighting was bitter and, to make matters even worse, there was yet another characteristic switch in the weather. Here forces of *Germania* faced encirclement after stumbling in heavy fog into some retreating Russian columns. A timely assault by another company of the regiment saw off the threat. The objective was to cross the neighbouring river but this plan was in disarray when the

Left: A map of Operation 'Barbarossa', and the subsequent Soviet counteroffensive in the winter of 1941. *Wiking* were part of Army Group South, attacking through the Ukraine towards Uman.

Russians blew the bridge. The hour belonged to SS *Sturmbannführer* (Major) Jorchel, the advance guard commander, who forthwith mustered the pioneer platoon for a crossing in inflatable rafts with covering artillery fire. Once the advance party had reached the opposite bank it was followed by the rest of the battalion whose assault parties fanned out to reach the town while others stormed the surrounding houses to prize out any enemy lurking there. Meanwhile the Soviets began digging in east of Satanov and throwing a ring of steel around the bridgehead, buttressed at nightfall, first by air reconnaissance, and then by bombs aimed at those of *Germania* still making the crossing.

During the night of 5 July, a temporary bridge was slung across the river which the Russians immediately tried to bomb. But by midday the bulk of German forces were across in such numbers as to beat back the enemy. They were later reinforced by the muscle of two motorized companies. When there were signs that the Russians were withdrawing, a fast battalion consisting of an infantry and a 'flak' platoon was dispatched in pursuit. However, the move proved too hurried and, in the face of mounting casualties, they were forced to withdraw and temporarily go on the defensive. Their plight was not helped by severe thunderstorms and rain which for a while rendered the roads impassable.

Meanwhile, a change of plan was in the process of being implemented by Gerd von Rundstedt, commander of Army Group South. Although Army Group South was poised to take the glittering prize of Kiev, he perceived that the railway network, vital for Soviet troop deployment, converged at the major junction of Uman, further south. This was a valuable communications centre which had links south to the Crimea; to secure it became a priority over Kiev, especially when the Soviet Marshal Semyon Budenny was under orders to concentrate a section of his forces there. On 10 July, the German attack in the south was unexpectedly altered from a push in the direction of Kiev, to Uman itself. To assist in the battles around the area, *Westland* was switched at speed south to Talnoye, northeast of Uman with a further battle group dispatched further east to Dnepropetrovsk. The SS divisions were detached from the melée.

After a series of running battles, a ring of steel was flung around the area of Uman on 3 August and trapped within it were three armies, over 100,000 men with a formidable array of tanks and guns. The pincer held. 1st Panzer, linking up with armoured elements of a Hungarian infantry division, clamped hard on 25 Russian divisions. By 1 August, the Red defences at Novo Archangelsk were breached and the Uman pocket seized. But the men of *Wiking* were learning that this was not a war that could be conceived in textbook military terms. Alongside Soviet forces were combatants who wore no uniforms and could be of any age. Men and women served with equal enthusiasm, members of a citizen army willing to harass and annihilate its enemy as best it could, even if this meant deliberately destroying its own homes and families in the process. Peter Neumann wrote at that time:

'One has to be very careful where one walks since the entire countryside is mined. Incautiously opening a door may set one of the infernal things off. In some places everything is a booby trap. The magnificent pistol lying on the floor conceals a wire connected to an explosive charge. In the harmless interior of a samovar, pounds of cordite are hidden, waiting to blow up. Jamjars, vodka bottles, even a well, the rope of which one is tempted to pull in order to get a drop of fresh water – they are all death traps to be steered clear of.

'Sometimes it's easy to spot the wires leading to the acid on the percussion cap. The difficult thing is to dismantle the contraption without being dispatched to a better world. The simplest system is, from safe cover, to toss in three or four hand grenades before entering any building. The explosion sets off the booby traps at the same time.'

By no means all the Russian soldiers matched the dedication of their civilian comrades. In those early days, there were instances of blind panic by the Red Army. In the aftermath of a tank battle at the town of Lvov, the men of *Wiking* did not need to take prisoners.

Left: This *Waffen-SS* man is seen toting an example of the best-known German weapon of World War II: the MP 38/40 series of submachine guns, of which more than one million were manufactured.

Every district they entered was already deserted. The Russians, along with their dead and wounded, had even carried away their spent shell and cartridge cases. Thrown into disorder by the German advance, the enemy had fled on foot, in carts and lorries, leaving only an overwhelming stink of filth and decay.

PROGRESS

Opposition from isolated pockets of resistance and guerrilla groups aside, the progress of the division's tanks over the dusty roads of the Ukraine from Dubno to the outskirts of Zhitomir was relatively unhindered. And all the while there were seemingly endless columns of Russian prisoners captured in the pocket of Lvov marching towards the rear. Abandoned tanks and guns cluttered the roads. Peter Neumann again:

'The tanks of the *Wiking* regiment slither down the steep roads leading to the banks of the Dnieper. Behind them at full speed come the armoured TCVs (Troop Carrying Vehicles), filled with troops, and performing a veritable slalom in their efforts to avoid the innumerable shell holes and carcasses of men and beasts that block the road.

The Reds, from the far side of the river, are desperately trying to stem this formidable onrush of tanks and infantry …

A continuous barrage, extending for miles, of ack-ack guns being used as antitanks is firing ceaselessly at our panzers. The latter are regrouping, awaiting the moment when the pontoons will make it possible for them too to cross the Dnieper …

As for us, we cling to the iron uprights of our armoured TCVs as we head for the bank. We are waiting to get within range before we open fire …

A hundred yards [100m] in front of us a lorry has just overturned and rolls over, probably eliminating one platoon of the antitank company. Thirty men, and not one escapes. A wounded man with both legs crushed begs us to finish him off. There's no time. The ground shakes, everything seems to disintegrate and disappear… A shell has just hit the front of our vehicle head on. It is a miracle any of us are alive.

There is death on every side. A hurricane of steel beats down on us as we painfully dig out the remnants of the lorry. Several men are trapped between torn bits of metal. But it's too dangerous here. We can't help them – we are less than five hundred yards [500m] from the Russian batteries.

I suddenly notice that I haven't got my MP40 any more. It's obviously buried under the wreck of the lorry. I snatch another machine pistol from the dead hand of a *Rottenfuhrer*, whose glazed and staring eyes can no longer see the terrible, mortal struggle all about us. The MP40 seems terribly heavy. I must have bruised my arm when the lorry turned over.

While running forward something suddenly occurs to me. I have no ammunition. God, what a fool! A few minutes later, taking advantage of a lull, I see a *Sturmann* who carries an impressive belt slung across his shoulders, and I help myself to a handful or two. I am now fully equipped for the Dnieper crossing.'

Elsewhere, *Wiking* forces were dangerously weak, particularly *Nordland*, obliged to strengthen a particularly weak bridgehead on the Dnieper, its motorized infantry impotent against strong attacks by Russian forces that were well prepared. In the area of a small bridgehead over the Dnieper at Dnjepropetrovsk there was a Soviet artillery school whose cadets, excellent shots with field gun and cannon, had plotted the entire district thus giving the Russians the edge when it came to pinpointing German targets. One of *Nordland's* men wrote:

'Every morning the Russians rushed the bridgehead and tried to crush it. A weight of artillery fire never before experienced rained down on the defenders' positions. They fought bitterly, refusing to yield a metre of ground. In these days, the Germans, Danes, Norwegians and Finns grew together into an exemplary European combat team. Morning after morning, they fought off with great bravery repeated Russians assaults. They were recognized by their *Wehrmacht* comrades as the bridgehead's strong supporting pillar in the uneven battle.'

The orders given to *Wiking* were to extend the bridgehead which needed strengthening at the town of Kamenka. Under unrelenting artillery fire, units of *Nordland*, *Westland* and *Germania* crossed the river at the point of the bridgehead and moved into position.

After briefings from the artillery commander, Major-General von Roman, divisional orders were issued for the attack which took place on 6–7 September and captured the heights of the town of Kamenka, taking over 5000 prisoners, thereafter stopping Russian interference with the bridgehead.

BOOBY TRAP

On the day of the attack, three members of the Division at one point took refuge in a hut directly in line with the Russian positions. It turned out to be a well-primed trap; trip wires set off mines and explosive charges. *Panzer Grenadiere der Panzer Division Wiking im Bild* quotes from an on-the-spot report: 'The explosion destroys the walls, and causes the hut to collapse. Company commander and NCO remain under the rubble lying wounded. Pressure against the leading platoon on the left becomes greater. The platoon commander takes his group back, one at a time under covering fire. The wounded are taken care of.'

The subsequent Order of the Day issued by *Brigadeführer* (Major-General) Steiner made clear that this had been a considerable achievement. In addition to the prisoners, no less than eight Russian divisions had been smashed in front of the bridgehead and other strong forces tied down. Steiner enthused:

'Men of the *WIKING* Division. Days of difficult fighting lie behind you. In heavy fighting the Division has repulsed daily enemy attacks, taken Kamenka, captured almost 5000 prisoners and since then has stood on the bridgehead as the unshakeable cornerstone of this important position. Over eight enemy divisions have been smashed before the bridgehead and strong forces tied down. So by your resolute defence you have prepared the way for our comrades to push east from the Dnieper.

... We stand ready for further action with our old fighting spirit. The division has become a symbol for the firm bonds uniting all the volunteers within its

ranks. Whether of German, Dutch, Danish, Norwegian or Finnish nationality, Division *Wiking* is for us all an expression of our unity and common fate. These units are worthy to take their place in the history of German soldiery … I know that the Division will hit the enemy hard in the coming days and add to its glory Heil to you, *Kameraden!*'

For such euphoria there was, at this stage of 'Operation Barbarossa', plenty of good cause. Hitler had defied the advice of his generals that the central drive on Moscow was the overwhelming priority and had focused on what he regarded as the bread basket of Russia, the wheat lands of the Ukraine. He reasoned this to be of more importance than the fall of the

Soviet capital. The wide areas of the steppe had presented superb opportunities to the tacticians of the panzer group of General von Kleist to show off their paces. The Russians had not reckoned on a penetration in such depth, resulting in the sealing off of the Soviet concentrations at Uman and Kiev, the latter ranked as the greatest military disaster in Red Army history. After Kiev, the industrial city of Kharkov, the fifth largest Soviet city which was destined to change hands four times during the war, was first taken by the Germans on 24 October 1941, using two infantry armies in pincer movements to the north and south.

But it was something of a paper victory: Stalin did not intend to turn Kharkov into another Kiev and had ordered the abandonment of the city. 'Barbarossa', Hitler reasoned, was heading for victory. He had felt confident enough to resume the attack on Moscow. Left out of the reckoning, however, were the twin spectres of the Russian autumn and winter. They pre-

Below: Russian prisoners of war in the early days of 'Barbarossa', with *Wiking* troops in the foreground. At this stage of the operation, many prisoners had been taken, and there was good cause for celebration.

sented a form of warfare that the Germans could never win, a truth seized on by General von Greiffenburg, Chief of Staff to the *Wehrmacht's* Twelfth Army who commented: 'The effect of climate in Russia is to make things impassable in the mud of spring and autumn, unbearable in the heat of summer and impossible in the depths of winter. Climate in Russia is a series of natural disasters.'

CLIMATIC PROBLEMS

Driving rain would strike into faces like steel rods and churn up the mud, causing any vehicle that ran off the roads to sink up to its axles. At one point movement of forces was less than 3km (2 miles) a day. As well there was a shortage of fuel and bread. Rain gave way to snow which froze the engines of vehicles. Available grease, oil and lubricants lacked modern-day cold-resistant

Above: A quick briefing before the unit moves on to its next objective. *Waffen-SS* soldiers were encouraged to be self-reliant and to take the initiative, which reduced the impact on a unit if its commander was incapacitated.

properties. More serious was the risk of malfunction by rifle or machine gun. Intense cold could make metal as brittle as glass. Slender firing pins would snap, rendering the weapons useless. But the cold weather could have advantages. When frost hardened the mud of summer, movement was restored to previously paralyzed parts of the front. Streams and lakes frozen by really hard frost could serve as auxiliary roads which was invaluable for heavy vehicles. Thick and hard snow proved reasonably bulletproof and, in at least one encounter by *Wiking*, it saved a patrol from ambush. An NCO of the *Wiking* Division wrote:

'A few days ago we carried out a reconnaissance patrol into the Russian zone. It was a beautiful clear day. On such days the visibility is quite unbelievable.

One can see literally for miles and every detail is pronounced and clear. I mention this because it had a bearing on the patrol.

From our form-up position we crossed open ground and then moved into a wide shallow depression. This was the limit of our first bound. We lay down in this and took up defensive positions, recovering our breath, before making the next bound which was a small wood. Our *Sturmführer* [Lieutenant] looked

for a long time. Through the glasses I was then able to pick out a white cloth which covered a hole in the snow wall of a trench and through which the machine gun had been fired.

This was something so surprising as to be completely abnormal. Ivan had the ability to camouflage his positions in such a way as to make him almost invisible and will spend hours removing every trace of his presence. Yet here he had left marks which were distinct, clear and unmistakable. Thanks to the slackness of one Red machine-gun group, the whole position, a trench system not marked on our maps, had been betrayed.'

FRESH OBJECTIVE

The men of *Wiking* prepared to strike at the area of Schachty, lying to the north, which it was essential to take before the winter bit hard. The signs of approaching winter were already there and troops were obliged to disembark from those vehicles that were still mobile and push them through the mud and snow. The plight of 14th and 15th Panzer Divisions was especially dire, since both were in danger of being seriously overstretched. All of which was in sharp contrast to early November, when the Germans had blasted their way forwards with apparent insouciance in the summer offensives. Now near Rostov, an advance guard of *Westland* had to reinforce one of the panzer divisions engaged in heavy fighting at Oktjabrisk, while contingents of *Germania* pushed towards Agrafenowka which was to the east of the Tusloff river and in a direct line north of Rostov. The Russians were harnessing the latest technology, showing the initiative they previously had lacked. One sign was the appearance of the fast, reliable and well-armoured T-34 tank, which was being deployed in ever-increasing numbers as replacements for obsolete and thinly armoured vehicles.

But this was a war of strange contrasts. Apart from their crack armour, the Russians could draw on a

through his glasses at a low ridge in front of which we would have to pass. He called to me and pointed to something on the ridge. I looked through the glasses and saw it immediately. Clearly in the bright sunlight there were long black streaks across the snow; the marks made by a machine gun which had been firing

source of military expertise with its origins centuries before. Thrown into the cauldron would be cavalry whose ranks were drawn from Cossacks and Kalmuks, people who had been born to the saddle and were highly mobile. Trained to fight as infantry, they used their mounts to cover vast distances, sometimes towing light artillery and mortar limbers. Their shaggy little Kirghil Siberian ponies had one advantage the Germans did not possess: the ability to withstand temperatures of minus 30 degrees. On the advance towards the Rostov area near the tiny village of Nowo-Krasnowka, a group of artillery, together with the forces of *Nordland*, found themselves facing a startling new phenomenon. An eyewitness (quoted in *European Volunteers*) described the experience:

'I happened quite by chance to look towards the range of hills 2–3 kilometres [1.25–2 miles] north of our position. At first I couldn't believe my eyes. In the name of heaven, what is that? A closed front of horsemen burst forth from the hills and stormed towards us. I nudged *Untersturmführer* [Lieutenant] Lindner who yelled "Alarm, Cossacks!" For a few seconds everyone was paralysed. Seconds seemed like an eternity. But then the spell was broken. *Untersturmführer* Lindner and I each ran to a gun and finally the first shots roared out in a direct fire. Meanwhile both of the anti-aircraft vehicles' MGs begin to hammer. The range decreases – 700, 600, 500 metres [700, 600, 500 yards]. Now all guns are firing. A terrible sight. Horses and riders plunge to the ground, yet the cavalcade continues to storm ceaselessly towards us. By the time they are 100 metres [100 yards] away, the attack has been so decimated that it no longer poses a serious danger. Still, 70–80 Cossacks reach our fire position swinging their *Saschka* (Cossack sabres) above their heads. The majority break through and disappear beyond the next hill; the rest have fallen in battle.

We are still quite numbed when the apparition has passed. Of the approximately 600 Cossacks, more than

Right: This *Kettenrad* (chain-wheeled vehicle) was employed primarily for transporting the *Waffen-SS* across sections of particularly rough ground, as shown here in what appears to be a propaganda photograph.

300 lay dead on the battlefield. Interrogation of the survivors revealed that the Russian commander thought that the troops in front of him were his own. By the time he recognized them as Germans it was too late to turn round, so he decided to try and ride over us. The destruction of this cavalry regiment belonging to Marshal Buddeny's army was entirely due to the devastating effect of our shells …'

ROSTOV ABANDONED

In the dying days of November there was another climatic freak: the weather turned a little warmer but the cold was replaced by thick fog. The overall situation was no happier. Kleist's tanks made it to the mouth of the Don on 21 November, bolstered by the propaganda machine of Josef Goebbels, which boasted that 'the gateway to the Caucasus' had been opened. According to one *Leibstandarte* man, the fall of Rostov was greeted by its inhabitants with 'tremendous enthusiasm'. As far as the Red Army was concerned, the truth was otherwise. First, the Germans

Above: Rostov on the Don, briefly captured from Soviet NKVD troops and then abandoned reluctantly by *Wiking* in the winter of 1941. It was to change hands twice more during the war.

had been slowed by antitank obstacles, ditches and minefields. *Wiking* troops faced, not Red Army soldiers, but their opposite numbers in the Soviet hierarchy: NKVD troops, the Soviet version of the *Waffen-SS*. These men fought hand-to-hand in the streets where they ripped up paving blocks to serve as thick barricades. Basements became repositories for scores of Molotov cocktails laced with phosphorus and petrol. Almost every door concealed booby traps and tripwires. Pillboxes spat fire amid flamethrowers, grenades, machine guns, rifles and bayonets. The

Right: Men of the *Freikorps Danmark* in 1941, a time when some 500 had volunteered. Those who joined the *Waffen-SS* were regarded as traitors by the Danes and their pension rights were removed, a move reversed by Himmler.

Wiking wounded were either bayoneted as they lay in the street or were dragged from troop carriers serving as makeshift ambulances. Within days the Russians had driven the Germans out of the town and they fell back to defensive positions across the Mius, leaving behind piles of dead. Against furious onslaughts, *Leibstandarte* and *Wiking* held on, but it was hopeless.

The severity of the winter had the effect of curbing the fighting along the entire length of the Russian Front. Any actions had one characteristic in common: they spelt actual or potential disaster for the Germans. In February 1942, the German lines were penetrated when the Russians launched an offensive with attacks along the front from Finland in the north to the Crimea in the south. Northwest of Moscow, the *Das Reich* Division, in the thick of the fighting, sustained around 11,000 casualties and, along with the Panzergrenadier Division *Leibstandarte,* was pulled out of the line for retraining in France.

Elsewhere that month, attention focused on the sorely threatened Leningrad front. Leningrad, formerly St Petersburg, was where Czar Peter the Great had sunk massive piles into the morass of the Neva estuary, at the cost of tens of thousands of lives, to build the fortress of St Peter and Paul. Then followed the Kronstadt naval base on one of the hundreds of islands in the Neva delta, and finally, palaces, boulevards and grandiose squares. But to Adolf Hitler it represented the hated cradle of Bolshevism to be 'wiped off the face of the earth. The further existence of this large city is of no interest once Soviet Russia is overthrown.'

Below: Members of the *Legion Norwegen* in the Soviet Union. Confidence in victory before the year's end had led to insufficient winter clothing being ordered, a problem that afflicted both the *Waffen-SS* and *Wehrmacht*.

Capitulation, reinforced the *Fuhrer*, was 'not to be accepted, even if offered'. It was Hitler's belief that Leningrad, if subjected to relentless terror raids, would cave in. General Manstein, sent to Leningrad in command of Army Group North, profoundly disagreed, believing that any attack on the city had been left too late and was a drain on resources. He favoured crossing the Neva southeast of the city and destroying the forces between there and Lake Lagoda. Supply routes would be cut off and the city isolated.

PROMISING PROSPECTS

In terms of achievements so far, German prospects looked promising. First had come the race by the *Wehrmacht* through the Baltic states. Four major rivers had been crossed, wrenching open a gap between the lakes of Peipus, Pskov and Ilmen. Army Group North and the iron fists of Sixteenth and Eighteenth Armies and General Erich Hoepner's Panzer Group 4 were poised to strike. The two Russian armies, under the command of General Fyodor Kuznetsov, were perceived to be seriously under strength, but the Soviets held the advantage in armour, particularly in 43-tonne (42.3-ton) KV-1 and 52-tonne (51.2-ton) KV-2 tanks with their 76.2mm (3in) armoured plating. Against this massive firepower German resources proved inadequate; tank could not be pitched against tank. The best options involved more caution and included the placing of explosives and the demolition of tank traps. These were achieved, but it led to delay for *Generalleutnant* George-Hans Reinhardt's XLI Panzer Corps in its drive for the broad Dvina river, which was eventually reached in early July. By the middle of the month, Reinhardt, who had been left to fret at the delay, finally reached the Luga river, the last major obstacle before Leningrad itself.

But it had not been achieved without help. In turning to the Finns, Hitler recalled that those territorial losses Finland suffered after the Winter War with Russia in November 1939 had been harsh, and so fears of a wholesale Soviet takeover were widespread. Forever cynical, the *Führer* recognized that such fears were worth playing on. Hitler was well aware that 400 or so Finns had been seconded at the start of World

Above: Men of the *Germania* Regiment. The failure to win victory in the East before the onset of winter was a disappointment to many, not least Hitler. Now the *Waffen-SS* had to fend off both the cold and the Red Army.

War II to 5th *SS-Wiking* and no time was lost in informing Finland that action was required to support their formation in the Leningrad area. The Commander in Chief, Field Marshal Mannerheim, showed his independence by biding his time. Then a Finnish division was there to besiege Hango on the south coast, while two corps advanced – one moving north of Lake Onega and one moving south – in a bid to trap Soviet troops against the water's edge before the frozen lakes could provide an escape route. But the Finns had no intention of dissipating their forces, of whose weaknesses they were well aware. Only a total of seven of their divisions were at full strength. Their keenest deficiency was in armour; every model of Finnish tank was inferior to the Soviet T-34.

ATTACK OVER THE LUGA

Amid heavy driving rain on 8 August, Army Group North burst from its bridgeheads over the Luga, which formed the outermost line of the Leningrad defences, the city itself being protected from the rear by the vast watery expanses of Lake Lagoda. Army Group North managed to secure Schlusselburg (later Petrokrepost) at the southern tip of the lake; the Finnish and German forces were separated by a mere distance of 64km (40 miles).

All the territory which had been lost in the Russo–Finnish winter war had now been rolled up; Vyborg was occupied on 29 August, and Terijoki on the old Soviet-Finnish frontier was occupied on 31 August. One more push was needed to reach the Leningrad suburbs. But Mannerheim now went no further with his territorial ambitions.

Above: No amount of intensive barrack-room training for eager young *Waffen-SS* volunteers could prepare them fully for the iron cold of the Russian Front, and frostbite claimed many of the ill-equipped Germans.

At one point during the Leningrad siege, men of *SS-Nordland* were patrolling around 1200m (0.75 miles) of territory stretching from the Gulf of Finland deep into the city itself. Olaf Lindvig, who was the commander of No 2 Company and then a young man of only 25 years old, would recall this episode extremely clearly after the war:

'I had been suffering from a touch of tuberculosis and I had been sent for treatment to a hospital in Riga. During that time a whole *Leibstandarte* battalion had received a severe mauling in the Leningrad area. The reaction of our division was immediate. There was hardly an hour that we didn't receive the order: "Clear out those Russians." The job was given to 2nd Company, but its commander had been wounded and I was told to step in which was a bit daunting because I was totally unfamiliar with the terrain.

The orders were that we were not to open the attack from the front, but to set up combat and reconnoitre groups which would be backed by infantry support. The strength of the patrols, which were organized by the company commanders, could range from eight to ten men or in some cases be of platoon strength.

Many volunteered for the patrols and they tended to be those who at home were hunting enthusiasts.

Below: A *Waffen-SS* volunteer during the advance on Leningrad. Despite the Germans' best efforts, the siege of the city would last into 1944, tying down large numbers of German troops wanted elsewhere.

They were undoubtedly among the best we had. At first, company commanders led each excursion, but this was a luxury we soon couldn't afford, particularly when in one disaster an entire patrol was struck by a Russian mine and the whole lot killed.

The Russians had set up a network of outposts and listening posts and the strength of their storm troopers seemed limitless. They seemed to have plenty of snipers whose aim was spot on. They would lie for hours, training their binoculars. They were so sharp that they could knock a man's head off the moment he put it above the trench. The easiest targets were young Norwegian reservists, green and wet behind the ears. Some were so trigger happy that they would sit on the edge of a trench and blast off their weapons. They didn't last long.

The Russian artillery also would send half-a-dozen or so bombers at a time to attack our rear areas. The best occasion was when two *Luftwaffe* fighters shot

down these nuisances and we were able to capture the crew after it baled out.

When we moved to Urizik which was much closer to Leningrad than our previous position, we had a combat role and the fighting got really nasty. It was now the turn of the Russians to get jittery because they reckoned that this area was particularly vulnerable to our attack. Our position was at Urizik, a suburban railway line ran along a high embankment. Our trenches were on the embankment's forward slope which meant that they flooded easily during this season of thaw. At one point we were forced back and the Russians, seizing the advantage, secured the trenches. The wet weather was vile but the Russians were helped by their American-style rubber boots which stretched from heel to crotch. This enabled them to move about more freely than had been the case with us.

It was decided to open the attack first from above, rather than head on. Our scouts had come across a deserted museum building and a 12-man team, armed with grenade launchers, scaled it rapidly to sight the weapons. Meanwhile we below had spotted a creek whose waters snaked through to within sight of the Russian positions. We followed its length to ... where we could open up comfortably when our turn came.'

TEXTBOOK ATTACK

'Coordination for the attack was textbook stuff. The leader of our assault troops fired a Very [flare] pistol which was the signal for the grenade launchers. The time was 13:00 hours on 2 May. Our troops on the ground then opened up with MG 34s, submachine guns, rifles and hand grenades. For these we had previously concocted a crude handle to which we attached five hand grenades in a single bundle. This was tossed into the enemy's bunkers and trenches. One of our volunteers was half Russian and half Norwegian and soon he was shouting to the Russians in their own language to put up their hands and come out. The heavy

Right: Victims of an artillery bombardment of Leningrad during the early stages of the siege of the city. The buildings in the background do not yet show significant battle damage, and the trams are still running.

machine guns were emptied into them as they broke out of their trenches and ran back towards the city. It was sheer slaughter, a horrific massacre.

I remember five of them who surrendered. They were miserable specimens. One was a commissar who had the Communist hammer and sickle on his helmet. I remember that he ripped off these and stamped on them in a blind rage. There were two others with a single Norwegian guard in charge. At one point our man took up some tobacco to roll himself a cigarette. The Russians stared at the tobacco hungrily, since they didn't have any. But in their pouches was some butter. A gentlemanly swap was agreed The prisoners were also persuaded to part with their rubber boots.

I was anxious to have a look at the trenches, following the assault. As I made my way towards them, an explosion sent me flying. I had stumbled either on a small mine or bomb, which could have been dropped

Above: A Soviet 85mm (3.35in) antiaircraft gun position in the harbour at Leningrad. As well as the repeated attacks by the *Waffen-SS* and *Wehrmacht*, the inhabitants suffered the regular attentions of the *Luftwaffe*.

from an aircraft. I lay on the ground and was conscious enough to see that one foot was dangling on a thread. Stretcher bearers stuck it together as best they could and I was carried to the company first aid post and then various hospitals and a number of operations in Germany. I was out of the war. Throughout my service I have to say that, even in the toughest conditions, medical facilities were first class.'

Right: In the ruined outskirts of Leningrad, a *Waffen-SS* observer scans the Russian front line positions with his binocular periscope. Using a binocular periscope enabled the user to judge distances.

HEAT AND INSECTS

Late in February 1942, the men of the *Norske* Legion had been summoned to the task of holding the Leningrad Front. Converging in their Junkers Ju-52 transports, their remit was to plug a front that stretched to Lake Lagoda, which was already buttressed by the Latvian legions and the Flemish battalions as well as a Spanish volunteer infantry division. The ability of the Norwegian fighters to resist the worst of the cold climate was indeed a major advantage, but this did not solve their problems entirely, as there were still the inevitable snipers' duels and clashes with scout parties.

The first offensive would involve an assault troop of a few dozen men. These fighters launched a hit-and-run attack in the area of the ruined town of Kiskino on the Neva river. This was within distant sight of the city of Leningrad. Withdrawal to temporary reserve behind the Constantinovka lines was then followed by a march to new objectives which had been chosen along the Leningrad Front, namely the positions of Hill 66 and the town of Pulkovo. Constant fire was exchanged with the enemy by 4th Company, which was under the command of *Haupsturmführer* (Captain) Berg.

There was increasing worry at the varying movements of the Russian troops which, it was felt, most likely pointed to an imminent attack. Reliable intelligence on this area was lacking. The decision to send out a raiding party proved disastrous. The party stumbled into a field peppered with mines, where Berg was killed, and those who survived were easily picked off with artillery fire.

As so often throughout the eastern offensive, changes in the weather proved almost as effective a foe to the Germans as the opposing combatants. With the approach of summer, the Norwegian talent for survival in a cold climate was now no longer relevant. Major adversaries in the swampy terrain from Leningrad to the Volkov river were the heat and the attendant mosquitoes. The Norwegians, fighting with comrades in the Latvian Legion, took the full brunt of a renewed Russian offensive. There was a on the whole futile bid by the Norwegian 14th Anti-Tank Company to halt the advances of the heavily armoured T-34 and T-52 tanks. The Norwegians' 3.7cm (1.46in) guns proved hardly a match for those of a Soviet Army that sometimes gave the impression of moving at will through the German lines.

Completely on his own initiative, *Oberscharführer* (Sergeant) Arnfinn, chief of a two-gun antitank battery which was stationed a few miles behind the lines at Constantinovka, swiftly took up blocking positions with his command near Novo Panovo. After the abandonment of one gun, yet another was hauled into a firing position and a sizeable Red Army infantry advance was held off until there was relief from a German police battalion. With the German troops counterattacking from the front, and in the meantime the Norwegians and Latvians moving in on the flanks, Soviet penetration forces were beaten off. Within 24 hours, the front lines had been restored and a substantial number of prisoners had also been taken.

As the months wore on, the *Norske* Legion was seen increasingly as the *Wehrmacht's* fire brigade, being sent to plug trouble wherever it broke out. In addition, during the closing weeks of 1942, the 14th Anti-Tank Company acted as the saviour of the Spanish Blue Division, which was now in severe trouble on the eastern part of the Leningrad Front. The action was at its fiercest near Krasny Bor, where one Norwegian battery was encircled by a wave of Russian tanks and then forced to spike its guns and flee to the woods. Under cover of darkness, the men of the battery slipped back to the command post of 2nd SS Infantry Brigade and, along with the 7.5cm (2.95in) gun crew of 14th Company, stemmed the Soviet advance in a successful bid to ease the plight of the Spanish SS.

But all too soon for the men of *Wiking* came a fresh assignment in new territory. This fresh assignment was to be the unenviable task of spearheading the attack on the oilfields of the Caucasus.

Right: This Norwegian *Unterscharführer* (Senior Corporal) displaying one variant of his country's sleeve badge. The Norwegians were perhaps at an advantage over their German comrades, being used to cold winters.

CHAPTER FOUR

THE CAUCASUS

Hitler's intentions to secure the oil resources of the Caucasus were dwarfed by the disaster of Stalingrad which ended the dream of pushing the enemy into the Volga. The Führer next urged major strikes to secure Kharkov before the launch of the summer offensive in the Kursk salient.

Both sides on the long and bloody Eastern Front were totally exhausted by the opening of the second year of World War II. The winter fighting had cost Hitler dear. A *Wehrmacht* report revealed that of a total of 162 combat divisions in the East, only 8 remained capable of offensive missions. The 16 armoured divisions could call on just 140 serviceable tanks, less than the normal allotment for a single division. Service morale had never been lower. Yet Hitler remained buoyant, arguing that his army, however depleted, had survived the century's coldest winter. Bolstered by the fact that he had assumed the position of Commander-in-Chief of the Army in addition to Supreme Commander of the Armed Forces, the Führer proposed to concentrate all his resources in the south and secure the oil of the Caucasus. Just before the start of the summer offensive, he told General Friedrich Paulus, commander of Sixth Army: 'If I do not get the oil of Maikop and Groznyy then I must end this war.' He argued that possession of these oilfields – the Maikop fields alone produced annually two-and-a-half million tons of oil – would serve to block the last main

Left: The 5cm (1.96in) mortar, shown being primed in this picture, was the leGrW 36 version, lighter than many of its fellows. Its effectiveness in combat proved limited and so it was gradually withdrawn.

route via the Caspian Sea and the Volga over which oil was able to reach central Russia.

FRESH PLANS

Envisaged was a two-pronged offensive. One arm would be extended eastwards in the area of Stalingrad to obliterate Soviet forces between the Don and Volga rivers, while the other would arrow towards the Caucasus. The proposal was greeted with scepticism by the army chiefs because of the distances involved: the two prongs, it was argued, would be too far apart to support one another. Chief of Staff Frank Halder pointed out that the *Wehrmacht* and *Waffen-SS* were short of half a million men for so ambitious a task. All reservations were contemptuously thrust aside. Securing the oil supplies was everything. 'My generals know nothing of economic warfare,' Hitler declared. Plans for the new offensive went ahead. As for manpower, the German High Command milked the Allies, satellites and foreign volunteers for additional forces. Above all, Hitler seized on the track record of the *Waffen-SS* to carry out a substantial expansion. Further plans included withdrawing the *Nordland* regiment from *Wiking* and using it as a cadre for a new SS division, *SS-Freiwilligen-Panzergrenadier-Division Nordland*. This was a cocktail of existing Germanic legions with western and southeastern European volunteers.

For Himmler, the new division looked like being the latest toy of the *Reichsführer-SS*. Himmler had burrowed among his ancient tomes and had come up with the name of *Warger* (Varagian). The Varagians, he earnestly explained to anyone who cared to listen, were Norse rovers who, in the 9th and 10th centuries, had invaded and colonized much of Russia. They had penetrated as far as Constantinople, where for the next five centuries a 'Waragian Guard' had been part of the household troops of the Byzantine emperors. But Hitler, to the extreme chagrin of the *Reichsführer-SS*, evinced scant interest in either Varagians or Byzantine nabobs. The 11th Division was dubbed *Nordland*, filled out with, besides *Wiking* men, ethnic Germans from other units and recruits from Hungary.

ESTONIAN VOLUNTEERS

A follow-up was the attachment to *Wiking* of a healthy number of Estonians. At first, Himmler had scruples about the formation of SS units consisting of

Above: The German summer offensive of 1942, driving towards the oilfields of the southern Caucasus after the capture of Rostov on the Don. However the terrain and stiff Soviet defence slowed the Germans' progress.

Estonians, and possibly Latvians and Lithuanians. While admitting that the idea was 'enticing', he saw it at first as being fraught with great dangers, not least because of the dubious racial strains he detected among natives of Baltic states. But the urgent need for manpower overcame these objections and it was not long before the *Reichsführer-SS* was changing his tune and tapping into the strong pro-German sentiment among Estonians. Their country had been assigned to the Soviet sphere of influence through an agreement between Germany and Russia in 1939. In the following year Estonia had been taken over entirely by the USSR. However, shortly after the start of 'Operation Barbarossa' the Germans had taken control of the territory and local irregular forces had joined in the fight against the Russians. Within weeks, Himmler was proudly displaying impressive recruitment figures: more than 200 Germans and 700 Estonians were within the Estonian Legion. Within four months, the figure for Estonians had swollen to 6500 and there was a welcome addition of 15,000 Latvians. An assembled group of Estonian candidates undergoing *Waffen-SS* training were inspected by the *Reichsführer* who declared: 'The Estonians really belong to the few races that can, after the segregation of only a few elements, be merged with us without any harm to our people. A nation of 900,000 Estonians cannot survive independently. As a racially related nation, Estonia must join the *Reich*.' Sufficient recruits were assembled at the German training camp at Debica in Poland to form three battalions. The result became 1st *Estnische SS-Freiwilligen-Grenadier-Regiment* (1st Estonian SS Volunteer Grenadier Regiment) of *SS-Panzergrenadier-Division Wiking*, brigaded in May with the addition of two regiments. The brigade was at first employed on anti-partisan operations within Estonia but was to find itself involved in what became an all too familiar 'fire-brigade' role.

In July a triumph for the Germans was the recapture of Rostov on the Don. On this occasion the Russians had lost heart and, in panic, had abandoned the city. Stalin meted out a terrible revenge to the Soviet generals and officers concerned; there were mass arrests and mass executions. Another boost had come at the end of June; Russian forces had taken the full impact

Above: If it was not the snow, it was the thaw, and then the inevitable mud. This *Wiking* truck, seen in Russia in early 1942 was, like so many others in the German fleets, totally unsuited to this terrain.

of General Hermann Hoth's Fourth Panzer Army, attacking from east of the city of Kursk. Ahead of the *Wehrmacht* and placed strategically on the Don was the industrial city of Voronezh that controlled road, rail and river traffic into central Russia from the west and south. Still further south lay the yet unconquered regions of the Ukraine and beyond that, the Caucasus. Here the men of *Wiking* fought in entirely novel battle conditions. In the north there had been flat roads and open countryside, but by contrast the country south of the Don contained some 190km (300 miles) of steppe. Crossing the steppe was the first stage before traversing one of the world's most formidable mountain chains, stretching between the Black and Caspian seas. It was a formidable proposition. Russian defence advantages seemed numerous. Countless large and small rivers flowed from the Caucasus into both seas, presenting obstacles which an experienced enemy could hold

with comparatively weak forces. In his *European Volunteers*, Peter Strassner describes territory which in the early summer was in total contrast to that which the men of *Wiking* had experienced in the Ukraine 'where the villages were prettier, the roads better and the countryside was covered with golden corn and red tomato fields'. As they progressed, troops were allowed to pause briefly, gorge on fruit and slake their thirst against the effects of the hot, dusty climate.

A crossing in inflatable craft was made of the 350km (563-mile) long Kuban river, which rose in the mountains of the Caucasus flowing northwest into the swampy delta before the Sea of Azov. *Nordland*, whose

progress so far had been with *Germania*, peeled off to take the key railway junction of Krapotkin, where on 7 August a Russian withdrawal was reported. The Division, at the head of LVII Panzer Corps, and under the command of Felix Steiner, arrowed southwest in the direction of Tuapse. This was followed by penetrations northwest and southwest of the Maikop region. In their retreat, the Russians had abandoned guns and vehicles but there was no time for the Germans to recover them in their headlong rush. The eventual conquest of the oilfield had its ludicrous aspect. The German High Command had ordered that a group of oil specialists and technicians was to follow the forces into the Maikop fields and ensure the maintenance of production. This motley group proved to be only of nuisance value and led Peter Strassner to record: 'What a strange frontline unit! The company, without any experience of combat, promptly ran into a Russian ambush in the Giaginskaja area and were shot up. In any case, there was no oil produced during the division's stay in this area.' This was hardly surprising, since the Russians had previously made a point of destroying most of the equipment.

CITIZEN ARMY

Prominent among the *SS* men in pursuit of the enemy was a battalion of Finns who had been incorporated the previous year into the *Nordland* regiment and had been assigned to *Wiking* Division. Earlier in the year its officers had attended the *SS-Junkerschüle Tölz* in Bavaria and the Battalion was now re-equipped with the newest armed vehicles. The Finns went into action at Linejuaja, helping to scatter VII Soviet Guards Cavalry Corps whose contingents melted into the rugged forest and mountains of the Caucasus. This was followed by a fresh anxiety. A member of *Westland* on guard duty in the area of Dadrowskaja was soon reporting renewed activity by those who had fled to the protection of these same mountains. There were signs of defences being

Left: A stuck *Wiking* motorcycle and its load in the mud caused by the spring thaw on the Eastern Front. Two *Wiking* troopers try to lift the vehicle out of the mud's embrace. Note the SS numberplate.

dug in the passes and increased activity by partisans who were ambushing munitions and supplies. By 25 August, the tanks of *Generaloberst* (Colonel-General) Ewald von Kleist's First Panzer Army were in sight of Mozdok, in the east of the Caucasus, around 80km (50 miles) from Groznyy, where all forces were urged to make the final push. A hastily assembled Russian citizen army, however, had begun building pillboxes, miles of trenches, anti-infantry and antitank obstacles. There the Germans were halted and they were to remain there through the autumn and winter. It was this winter which struck at Norwegian volunteer Ornulf Bjornstadt of *Germania*, who was positioned with his platoon on a stretch of high ground which was located in the eastern Caucasus.

'When I settled down for the night in my foxhole which was on a hillock, it was raining hard. The temperature dropped and the water trapped in the foxhole iced over while I slept. When I awoke it was iron hard and I was literally frozen to one wall. I couldn't move at all and my left side was totally paralysed. There was a bunker not far away where earlier there had been an attack by mortars which did plenty of damage, killing our company commander and wounding a lot of our men. Because of that there were doctors around and one managed to get to me after he heard me yelling. The only way to get me down the hillock was astride a motorcycle combination and I was bumped along until we reached a small town which had a hospital and hydro originally used by senior Communist officials and now occupied by us.

It was luxury to be between clean white sheets and the treatment was marvellous. There was Norwegian staff, including nurses. I was in high fever when I arrived and then I became crippled with rheumatism and it was a full month before I was able to be sent back to my unit which was in sight of a small Georgian village near the town of Osnokitsa. This was wooded country. The Elbrus, the highest mountain in the Caucasus region, towered above us. We set up a bunker in an abandoned house, establishing our mortar positions with infantry support, mine was near a creek – ideal because beyond was flat land leading to the village and it was good for observation.

I was not on night duty at that time which was lucky. One night there was a Russian scout patrol right in the path of my mortar position. Our men opened up. Next morning I discovered the body of a Russian officer slumped across my bunker. He had been caught in a spurt of machine-gun fire.

The enemy was very active, striking out from the village again and again, mostly by day. The latest mortar grenades were very effective. They would land on the flat then proceed to bounce up into the air before exploding with a deadly cascade of shrapnel splinters.

When we took Red Army prisoners we put them to good use, mostly in digging trenches. I remember one wretched lad who was quivering with fear when we took him. He looked desperate and told me he wanted to be my friend. I took pity on him and put him to work as the company's cook. He had that job for about three months before I turned him loose to get back to his own lines. What happened to him after that I don't know.'

On the wider front, a new obsession gripped Hitler. As well as intent on securing the Caucasus, he was also focusing on the capture of the city of Stalingrad, the key rail and river transport centre on the Volga's west bank. But before that there was another worry. The Russians were building up powerful forces to attack on a sector of the river Donetz and the Germans lacked the strength to hold them back. The spearhead of the key thrust was in the hands of Lieutenant-General Markian Popov's Armoured Group which, after penetrating Krasnoarmeyskoye, was hell bent on reaching Stalino (later Donetsk). As taut as coiled springs were 145 T-34s and a further 267 tanks waiting to lead the attack. The situation was assessed coolly by Manstein: facing Popov was XL Panzer Corps of General Sigrid Henrici, 7th and 11th Panzer Divisions and parts of 33rd Infantry Division, newly arrived from France. Then had come the order to *Wiking* to race from the Caucasus to combat the threat presented by Popov.

Right: A *Waffen-SS* machine-gun crew in action in the Soviet Union. These men would have been familiar with the 7.92mm (3.1in) MG 34 and MG 42, both excellent machine guns firing around 750 rounds per minute.

'STALIN ORGANS'

Wiking was told to switch from the Caucasus in response to a teletype message which read: 'The Commander WIKING Div: The entire Army looks to your Division. You have the task of paving the way for the Army towards Groznyy. I expect your armoured spearhead to be at Ssagopschin this evening at 18:00 hours, signed von Kleist.' Although Ssagopschin was indeed captured, this did not lead to the desired breakthrough towards Groznyy. Steiner advocated the seizure of what he saw as a far more important objective. Without securing the mountain city of Malgobek, there could be no guarantee that the forward echelons of *Wiking* would be able to hold their positions. The attack on the Malgobek ridge would be the responsibility of *Germania* on the south slope, with *Westland* serving as a reserve. On the night 4/5 October, the units moved into the assembly area, and the attack

Above: In the summer sun of 1942, these men of the *Wiking* Division in Russia are seen preparing a 15cm (5.9in) SiG 33 gun for firing at the enemy. That month had seen the capture of Voronezh on the Don.

began at 04:30 hours. Above the SS echelons a bank of Stukas screeched above the city, whose western areas were secured. But the Germans barely had time to breathe before the Russians riposted with a heavy tank attack along the Grusinischen highway. On *Germania's* southern flank came fire from *Nordland*, slowing the Soviet advance. A Divisional messenger reported in his diary on 29 September: 'A damned shitty mess in these days. We lack heavy artillery and above all air support. The right flank is open, it is reported – according to statements by a deserter, there is only an enemy security force there. We are terribly filthy. The little coffee is scarcely worth drinking.'

The Russians brought up a fresh division to be deployed east of Malgobek, reinforced by the multi-barrelled batteries that fired rocket-propelled mortars with devastating effect and which the Germans nick-named *Stalinorgen* ('Stalin organs') because of their sound. Peter Strassner assessed the situation bluntly: 'Continuing with the attack under these conditions would have been senseless, since the initiative appeared to have passed to the Soviets. In any case, there were insufficient German forces to carry out a large scale operation against distant Groznyy.'

One more try was made by the Finnish Battalion which, working with *Nordland*, was ordered to take the commanding height of Hill 701 which lay behind Malgobek and which small units had unable to reach. Assigned to the latest attempt was an assault troop under the command of *Obersturmführer* Tauno Pohjanletho. Mortar and heavy weapon support came

from 12 Company, whereas backing for the assault on the hill itself was provided by a panzer company. The firepower from the Russians was merciless, but the attack by the Finns, launched deliberately without an artillery barrage, came as a surprise. Pohjanletho's men put three antitank guns out of action with hand grenades. Three T-34s were set on fire by the panzers. As the attack wore on, Finn casualties mounted, along with those of the men of *Nordland*. The bid for the hill became a matter of close range conflict between tanks. At the end of it all, the Soviets were forced to transfer their main thrusts further south. It was scant consolation for what was happening elsewhere.

Below: *SS-Gruppenführer* **(Lieutenant-General) Felix Steiner (centre, with peaked cap) seen here with senior staff of** *Wiking.* **Steiner incurred the jealousy of General Hausser, who described him as 'Himmler's baby'.**

Wiking faced a fierce crisis when it became clear that it was increasingly difficult to hang on to its gains at Ssagopschin, let alone press forward. A breakout entailed a forced march southwards towards Alagir, a loss of valuable time. Subsequently upgraded to 5th *SS-Panzergrenadier-Division Wiking*, Steiner's force now faced increasingly tough opposition, reinforced by units of the NKVD who fought with a ruthlessness that the *Waffen-SS* could both recognize and respect. By the end of December 1942 the Germans were obliged to pull out of the Alagir area entirely. Around this time, Hitler's illusions about the likely course of the war were seemingly shared by General of Infantry Kurt Zeitzler, the new Chief of the Army General Staff who, in a meeting with Steiner, expressed confidence in the way in which the German offensive was being conducted.

However, the same could not be said for Franz Halder, Zeitler's predecessor, who had been sacked for daring to question that which he called Hitler's 'pathological over estimation of his own strength and criminal under estimation of the enemy's'. Halder had faced the Supreme Commander with some inconvenient facts. According to a reliable report, Stalin was still able to muster a total of from one to one-and-a-quarter million fresh troops in the region north of Stalingrad and west of the Volga, not to mention half a million men in the Caucasus. Furthermore, Russian output of front-line tanks amounted to around 1200 a month. Halder later recalled: 'Hitler flew at the man who was reading [the report] with clenched fists, and foam in the corners of his mouth and forbade him to read any more of such idiotic twaddle.' With the removal of Halder and his replacement by Zeitler – 'little more than the *Führer's* office boy', as described by the American writer William Shirer – any effective opposition to the Supreme Commander melted away to become a total silence.

Hitler's plan was for Sixth Army under General Friedrich Paulus to slice through the north of Stalingrad, to be followed by General Hermann Hoth striking from the south. The final assault would be by Paulus's army sweeping in to push the remaining Russian defenders into the Volga. It was true that the Germans succeeded in capturing 90 per cent of the city, but the remaining 10 per cent allowed the Russians to launch their crucial counteroffensive. Stalingrad's agony stretched over two months, during the course of which the city became – in the words of an officer of 24th Panzer Division – 'an enormous cloud of burning blinding smoke … a vast furnace lit by the reflection of the flames'. Sick, frozen and demoralized Germans were forced to eat the brains of dead horses just to survive. At the end of January 1943, the Sixth Army shuffled out into almost certain death in the Russian prisoner-of-war cages. Only 5000 of these men would ever see their homeland again.

NO RESPITE

By now, German-held territory was so dramatically overrun that it threatened the lines of communication of Army Group Don, which included Hoth's Fourth Panzer Army. Suddenly, Rostov was assuming the importance once attached to Stalingrad. More than one-and-a-half million men stood at risk. Stunned and bludgeoned, the Axis divisions were forced to fall back in the direction of the Dnieper while Russian armies poured into the Donetz Basin.

Wiking, which was soon due to be under the command of *SS-Brigadeführer* and *Generalmajor der Waffen-SS* (Major-General) Herbert Gille in succession to Felix Steiner, who had been appointed to command III Panzer Corps, had to face the truth that on the eastern Caucasus, the operation against Groznyy had been a total failure. Movement in the Black Sea coast sector was out of the question. Hitler's forces there were now immobilized due to lack of manpower and also, now predictably, the rigours of the Russian winter. On 14 February, Rostov had to be abandoned, and the city was entered by – among others – Soviet Military Council Member Lieutenant-General Nikita Sergeyevich Khruschev, who reported to Moscow: 'Over Rostov, the citadel of the quiet Don, the victorious Red Soviet Banner once again proudly flies.'

Right: Observation being carried out by a member of *Germania* on the Russian Front in the summer of 1942. This was the year in which Hitler ordered simultaneous operations against Stalingrad and the Caucasus.

FATIGUE

5th SS-Panzer-Division *Wiking* was in the throes of a desperate bid to dislodge the enemy from Krasnoarmeyskoye in the Ukraine. The Soviets were not the only enemy. Desperate fatigue came once again to plague the Division and its components worn out by the heavy demands of fighting in the Caucasus, on the Don and on the Mius. But the signal from Manstein brought no respite: 'Strong enemy – Popov's Armoured group – advancing across Donets at Izyum in southerly direction towards Krasnoarmeyskoye. *Wiking* will wheel to west immediately. Objective: tie down Popov's Armoured Group.' Popov's spearheads had swept south in a powerful thrust, creating a dangerous gap between First Panzer Army and Army Detachment Lanz. *Wiking* and XL Panzer Corps had a role in intercepting the thrust at certain points. Scandinavian and Dutch volunteers from *Nordland*, *Germania* and *Westland* bunched together in a bid to stop Popov's spearheads and press them together, but in question was how long, in their deeply weakened state, they could hold out. The SS men were assailed at one point by around 12 tanks with mounted infantry which were shot up in the village of Rovny. A Stuka assault on one of the enemy positions nearly ended in disaster when an advancing SS company was in danger of being annihilated; its aerial recognition signal saved it. Ornolf Bjornstad's *Germania* battalion dug in to aid the battle against Popov's advancing forces:

'I had returned from leave to rejoin my unit on the Kalymken Steppe in the Ukraine and it was bitter cold. Fighting was extremely difficult for both sides because the weapons became frozen stiff. Our mortars were more or less all right but our machine guns hopeless. We constantly had to rush into a nearby abandoned house to heat them. Luckily, we were well served with warm clothes, particularly furs and overcoats. Nevertheless, there were the inevitable casualties from frostbite.

Left: *Hauptsturmführer* (Captain) Oeck stands proudly with a *Wiking* crewmember before his Marder II tank destroyer, in July 1942. The Marder used the captured Soviet 7.62cm (3in) gun on a Panzer II chassis.

Left: A rare moment of reflection for this member of
Wiking **in Russia in July 1942. During May, the Red Army**
had once again gone over to the defensive as the
Germans launched their summer offensive.

Above: The Caucasus proved to be difficult going for the
units of Army Group A, which included *Wiking.* **The lack**
of roads, hilly terrain and fast-flowing mountain streams
hindered the Germans' progress.

We were no longer in a defensive position. We were
urged forward and ordered to attack ceaselessly
because of the threat from Popov's forces which were
trying to drive a wedge between us and some Italian
and Romanian troops.

Although we were motorized, our lorries frequently
seized up in the cold, so were obliged to abandon
them and where possible blow them up. This meant
piling as many men as we could into a single lorry
which was an added hazard on the icy roads.

When we reached the Donetz we dug in at a point
on the river with the Russians on the other side directly opposite us, but their's was partly a wooded area and
we couldn't see them properly. We sent out scout
patrols but the Germans were often no good because
they were not natural hunters and seemed incapable of
moving silently.

Among the prisoners we took were four Tartar
renegades who said they would be willing to work for
us so we set them to dig trenches. They shared the
same bunker as a *Wehrmacht* artillery group where
loaded machine pistols were hung on a post.
Overnight the Tartars seized the weapons and slaugh-
tered everyone in the bunker. Then they melted back
into the Russian lines. We were forbidden to have any
more prisoners in the front line after that.

That line was at the edge of these woods which were heavily mined and patrolled day and night by the Soviet scouts. Our intention was to attack west but before we could move we had to deal with these Ivans whose command post and billets were in a nearby village. At this time we got a new commander who came to us from *Westland* and ordered an immediate all-out assault.

As we advanced, we were puzzled by what seemed all of a sudden to be half-hearted Russian defence.

Above: Herbert Gille, who replaced Felix Steiner as the commander of SS-Panzer-Division *Wiking*, seen after his promotion to *Gruppenführer* (later *SS-Obergruppenführer*) *und Generalleutnant der Waffen-SS* (Lieutenant-General).

Right: An advance by *Wiking* armour in July 1942. A lot seemed to be going right for the German forces, with the capture of Voronezh on the Don, and further triumphs for Hoth's panzers to the southwest.

Their troops seemed content to let off only light artillery. When we got within attack distance – some 100 to 200 metres [100–200yd] – we found out why. Around a dozen tanks came roaring out where 2nd Company was positioned on the left. Our comrades there had no chance. The tanks drove over them. They were crushed to death. My company survived because we happened to be concealed in a hollow on the right Through his binoculars our commander saw the attack and soon our 8.8 [3.46in] cannons were in position and we got many of those Russian tanks through their turrets.

A runner who had managed to get near the village from a small valley on our right alerted us to a small machine-gun post. We peeled off from the attacking tanks and made for the sector in an all-out push, firing all the way from a small dry culvert and capturing the machine-gun post. I have two abiding memories of that time. One was the sight of a junior officer of ours running like hell and shooting at the same time. Then he got a bullet through the head. He turned round 180 degrees before he fell but until he hit the ground he didn't stop firing.

Above: Another advance by *Wiking* forces through verdant countryside in the summer of 1942. Alongside the *panzergrenadiers* is a Panzer III, which by this stage was becoming increasingly outdated as a combat tank.

Then there was this gigantic haystack in our path. There would have been nothing unusual in that if the haystack hadn't suddenly started to move and from it emerged this T-34. The tank drew level with the village cemetery and it was from there that a young *Obersturmführer* (Lieutenant) appeared, suddenly rushing forward and slapping a magnetic mine on the tank.

A bit later I was crouching in the culvert with my mortar in position behind me and through my binoculars I could see the enemy bunched ahead. They made a fine target, particularly one cannon I had my eye on. I was just about to line up the cannon when there were a number of loud "pings" by the side of me and, thinking they were Russian, I rolled over to get out of the way as fast I could. Then I saw the muzzle of this 7.5[cm (2.95in)] antitank cannon but not before I had taken the full force of powder on the cheek from the muzzle blast. Our man who had fired had concentrated on lining up the enemy through his telescope and had not seen me. I was angry because he had shot up the gun I had wanted for myself. I was stone deaf for a long time after that.

Next, we could see the Russians retreating at speed up the slope of a hill. So we fought our way into that by now abandoned village and had a brief rest. Then one of our *Obersturmführers* appeared, asking to see me. After congratulating me warmly, he told me that I had been granted a special place on an officers' training course at Bad Tolz. But I told him that I'd had enough, having volunteered only for one year, but in fact had stayed on for two and a half. He protested that I would be leaving some good comrades behind and maybe we could discuss the whole thing over a bottle of cognac. When that was finished he gave a broad grin and, confessing his joke, produced from his pocket a shoal of documents. They were my discharge papers.

As soon as I was able, I made the difficult journey home via Germany and on to Norway but not before I learnt that we had helped to stem General Popov's advance.'

POPOV SLOWED

But this, it turned out, was now hardly sufficient, particularly as Popov had succeeded in cutting the railway from Dnepropetrovsk to Stalino and was itching to push still further south to Mariupol on the Sea of Azov. It was an advance that had to be halted. The men of *Nordland*, *Germania* and *Westland* who had survived the fighting in the Caucasus, on the Don and on the Mius, were in no physical condition to move at speed. In addition, there was a chronic shortage of armour. From his position south of Krasnoarmeyskoye, *Obergruppenführer* (General) Gille employed a clever ruse that could have had its origins, not in a 20th century war, but in the more primitive skirmishes of the old American West. Success depended on skilful and flexible gunnery. Ceaseless searching and sweeping fire from the batteries, suggesting there was massive

Below: *Reichsführer-SS* **Heinrich Himmler watching a demonstration of armament capability by SS-Division** *Wiking* **around September to October 1942. The event is being photographed for propaganda purposes.**

firepower behind it, badly rattled the Russians, who had the impression that their enemy was present in greater numbers than in fact was the case. Popov's advance slowed, giving *Wiking* the chance to strike at Krasnoarmeyskoye from east and southeast. The sorely needed assistance came from 7th Panzer Division which had been holding the town of Slavyansk. It was allowed to evacuate and move into the Krasno-armeskoye area, while further forces from the area were freed for action. Stalin's intention had been that his armies would reach the Dnieper to prevent cross-ings by the fleeing Germans, and annihilate Manstein's Army Group in an operation to rival Stalingrad. It was a dream soon to be shattered by the additional inter-vention of Fourth Panzer Army whose corps drove towards the retreating Russians, encircling them for annihilation before they reached the Donetz. It put paid to six tank corps, ten rifle divisions and half-a-dozen independent brigades and had been aided by the sleight of hand initiative of Gille and of *Wiking*.

Above: Grenadier volunteers like these men from *Wiking* in Russia in October 1942 fought well, but discontent was seething in the ranks, due to the cavalier treatment meted out by their German *Waffen-SS* superiors.

All attention was soon focusing on the threat to Kharkov. Between 11 and 15 March there was vicious street-fighting to secure the beleagured city with a heavy toll on the resources of *Leibstandarte, Das Reich* and *Totenkopf* before the latter enveloped the area to the north of a city that had been destined to see-saw between German and Russian ascendancy. As it turned out, this triumph was brief, but it nevertheless acted as adrenalin for the SS forces.

There had also been a role for elements of *Wallonien* from Belgium, whose units within months were to be absorbed into *Wiking*. A graphic account of Germany's short-lived triumph comes from Leon Degrelle, who was undoubtedly the most charismatic of the Belgian volunteers:

'The Russians defended themselves with marvellous courage. Our machine guns battered their defences. The German artillery poured hundreds of shells on them with incredible precision, hitting the enemy bunkers dead centre. We saw the shelters blow up … The Russians constantly came back, dug themselves into the ruins, reorganized their positions …

The German Stukas intervened. More than 60 Stukas wheeled above our heads! Sixty-four to be exact, for our section alone. It was grand. The whole sky sang with man-made power …'

UNPLEASANT SURPRISE

Degrelle also recalled an incident when the legion was dug in at the village of Blagodoch near Kharkov:

'We drew our water from the village well. We sent a man armed with a hook attached to a heavy rope to search the bottom of the well. The hook soon caught on what we all thought was the bucket. It seemed to have become awfully heavy, though, and it took the strong arms and backs of several men to haul it in again. At last our catch emerged: a Mongol, huge, hideous, half-rotted, his belt hooked to our rope. We'd been drinking him for weeks …'

As for *Wiking* itself at this time, praise had been passed to the troops by an Order of the Day from SS-Panzergrenadier Division HQ. It said in part:

'Ater a long and difficult fighting withdrawal, necessary because of the serious situation on the Don front,

Below: All that intense barrack-square training received back in Germany makes sense. Deep in the Caucasus during 1942, these men of a *Wiking* machine-gun unit rush forward under cover of a smokescreen.

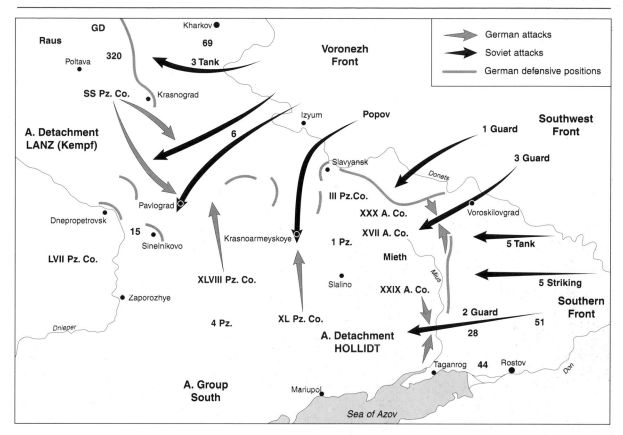

GD
Raus
Kharkov
Poltava
320
69
3 Tank
Voronezh Front
SS Pz. Co.
Krasnograd
Izyum
Popov
1 Guard
Southwest Front
3 Guard
A. Detachment LANZ (Kempf)
6
Slavyansk
III Pz.Co.
Donets
Voroskilovgrad
Pavlograd
XXX A. Co.
Dnepropetrovsk
15
Krasnoarmeyskoye
XVII A. Co.
5 Tank
Sinelnikovo
1 Pz.
Mieth
LVII Pz. Co.
5 Striking
Zaporozhye
XLVIII Pz. Co.
Slalino
XXIX A. Co.
Southern Front
Dnieper
4 Pz.
XL Pz. Co.
2 Guard
51
A. Detachment HOLLIDT
28
Taganrog **44** Rostov
Don
A. Group South
Mariupol
Sea of Azov

German attacks
Soviet attacks
German defensive positions

the Division has turned and struck decisive blows against an enemy which previously had been scarcely hindered. Today we stand once again on the Donetz, the Russian Popov Tank Army is smashed and the Russian 1st Guards Army and 6th Army are in retreat. The German soldier has triumphed once again.'

On the southern sector of the Eastern Front there was a short lull and with it came the chance for the Germans to consolidate their positions. Hitler's attention had by now fastened on an area that extended north from Belgorod, lying northwest from Kharkov, to the distant area of Orel. In the centre was a huge salient which, if taken, would help to regain the German initiative on the Eastern Front.

Left: In his rough winter clothing and thick gloves, this *Waffen-SS panzergrenadier* watches the enemy front line for any movement, holding his MP40 submachine gun close to him.

Above: In late February 1943, Manstein faced a massive Soviet breakthrough. Army Detachment Hollidt on the Mius faced three Russian armies. A further thrust came from Popov's Armoured Group south to the Sea of Azov.

Furthermore, it could be possible to entrap the cream of Red Armies, and annihilate those very forces which had inflicted on the Germans the humiliation of Stalingrad, as well as the defeat at the Don, during the previous unforgiving winter.

Indeed, a push back to the Don – and perhaps even the Volga – could be followed by a swing up from the southeast in order to seize Moscow. The salient was at Kursk, a substantial industrial city, from where intelligence sources had informed Hitler that there was an enormous build-up of Soviet field forces. Hitler's plan for the Kursk offensive was codenamed *Zitadelle* (Citadel), and it was the setting for what was to be the greatest tank battle in history.

CHAPTER FIVE

DEBÂCLE

Hitler's failure at Kursk sowed the seeds of his ultimate defeat. In addition, morale within the ranks of *Wiking* slumped disastrously, and was further exacerbated by the departure of the Finnish contingent. A fresh obsession gripped the *Führer*: to hold onto the salient at Korsun.

Determination to offset the reverses of 1943, and above all the defeat at Stalingrad, led Hitler to search for the grand flourish which would once and for all annihilate the Russians, thus preventing the possibility an enemy breakthrough to the Ukraine and on to the Crimea. For the scene of a spectacular *Blitzkrieg*-style pincer movement, Hitler seized on the Kursk salient. This was a bulge in the front line north of Kharkov, protruding as a giant fist into the German lines. Here Hitler planned the offensive, with forces including *Leibstandarte, Das Reich* and *Totenkopf* within II SS Panzer Corps. In all, 50 German divisions, including 16 panzer and motorized, had converged for an operation that was intended to achieve surprise with the maximum concentration of forces pushing on a narrow sector. However, virtually from the start, the Germans were on a hiding to nothing. There had already been a pre-emptive strike by the Russians at dawn on 5 July when they launched their massive artillery attack. This came after a warning by their spies that an assault on the salient, which ran a distance of 255km (160 miles), was imminent.

Left: A hurried conference on the Eastern Front before launching a fresh attack against the Red Army. The Kursk offensive was to prove Germany's last chance to defeat the Soviet Union.

At 03:30 hours, the offensive began. Kursk proved an unmitigated disaster for Hitler. Around one-fifth of the 500,000 men of the 17 panzer divisions with their newly issued Tiger tanks were wiped out, victims of a slaughter that was reminiscent of the very worst battles of World War I. The true extent of German fatalities has never been confirmed, but it is thought to be around 100,000. Russian losses were subsequently put much higher. The Red Army had benefited from three key advantages: advance intelligence, deep defences, and a vast pool of reserves; they could afford the casualties. On 4 August, the Germans had been pushed out of Orel with the Soviet offensive spreading along the entire Front. The offensive against the salient lasted eight days before Hitler summoned Field Marshals von Manstein and von Kluge to his East Prussia headquarters with the blunt declaration: 'I am obliged to suspend Citadel.'

IMPACT OF KURSK

Although *Wiking* had not taken part, the debâcle of Kursk impacted on the Division because, following this reverse, the fortunes of war overall for the Germans changed irrevocably. The days when the *Wehrmacht* and SS could surge ahead with minimum opposition belonged to history. The horrific casualty figures meant that, more than ever, there was a desperate need for ruthless and aggressive men to reinforce the ranks of this flexible SS outfit. Such manpower was becoming increasingly difficult to find. As well as sapping morale, the defeat at Kursk further exacerbated a growing problem within the *Waffen-SS*. There were growing complaints emanating from the foreign echelons that the glowing promises made in the early days by Himmler and others when seeking volunteers had not been kept. Young men who had been willing enough to sign up for one year's service found their applications for discharge were ignored and that they were being treated as enlisted men. Others who, understandably enough, wanted to serve with their own nationalities were shunted around without consultation as general replacements for all SS units. Particularly discontented were *Wiking's* Danes and Norwegians, who reacted by the simple process of reporting sick, then taking advantage of convalescent leave at home to slip across the Swedish border, thus avoiding any further service. In March 1942, Steiner had reported that two men from *Wiking* had gone so far as to desert to the Russians! However, all of this scarcely surprised Hitler himself who, right from the start of the war, had been irritated by Himmler's constant nagging about expanding the forces of the *Waffen-SS*. In the same year, over a dinner with the *Reichsführer-SS*, Hitler had proclaimed:

'We must not make the mistake of enlisting in the German Army foreigners who seem to us to be worthwhile fellows, unless they can prove that they're utterly steeped in the idea of the Germanic *Reich*. I'm sceptical about the participation of all those foreign legions in our struggle on the Eastern Front. One mustn't forget that, unless he is convinced of his racial membership of the German *Reich*, the foreign legionary is bound to feel that he is betraying his country.'

It had become vitally necessary to stop the rot. German senior officers and NCOs were assigned bigger training and disciplinary roles in the foreign

Right: New recruits to the *Legion Wallonien* swear an oath of loyalty to Adolf Hitler during a ceremony in Brussels on 3 March 1943. With the tide of the war turning against Germany, fresh manpower was urgently needed.

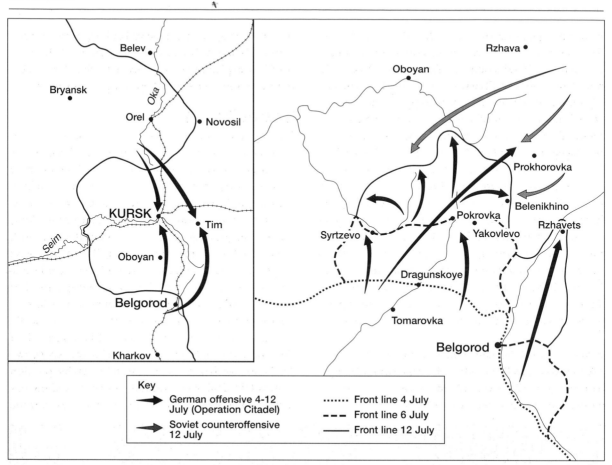

Key

➤ German offensive 4-12 July (Operation Citadel)

➤ Soviet counteroffensive 12 July

······· Front line 4 July

- - - Front line 6 July

——— Front line 12 July

legions. Himmler sanctioned measures to correct the worst abuses, which included allowing the release of men whose enlistment had expired.

LACK OF TANKS

Crises for the *Reich* on all fronts increased with the invasion of Sicily in July 1943 and then, two months later, the capitulation of Italy. Hitler rushed a portion of the SS Panzer Corps to the west. The most drastic regrouping centred round the newly established SS-Panzergrenadier-Division *Nordland,* whose three regiments were strengthened by transfers from *Wiking* and the inclusion of native Germans. In the east, there was an urgent need for increased steel. Seven *Waffen-SS* panzergrenadier divisions – including *Wiking,* which had originally been partly armoured motorized infantry – had become full SS panzer divisions. All

Above: The German 1943 summer offensive at Kursk took place without *Wiking*. The right-hand map shows a close-up of II SS Panzer Corps' attack in the southern sector of the Kursk salient.

were backed by the very latest that battle technology could provide in the way of tanks, self-propelled artillery and mechanized infantry.

In the wake of 'Citadel', a fresh Red Army counteroffensive was launched on 2 August after a massive artillery and air bombardment. The key centre of Belgorod, north of Kharkov, fell four days later. Around Kharkov itself, *Wiking* was back in the frame and, along with *Das Reich* and *Totenkopf,* was thrown into the cauldron to prevent the final loss of the city. Hitler's mantra was predictable: 'Kharkov must be held.' In the scorching days of autumn, with thick dust clouds hanging over the roads, the advance rolled on. The vehicles of the 3rd Panzergrenadier Regiment reached the Feski collective farm about 24km (15 miles) northwest of Kharkov, where vast German supply dumps had been set up in happier times. There were huge amounts of alcohol, tobacco and tinned food, all of which were hastily commandeered, with the exception of vodka, shunned by the *Wehrmacht* in favour of cognac, port and Chianti. Paul Carrel, in *Scorched Earth: The Russian–German War 1943–1944*, wrote: 'No one, of course suspected that this despised Russian vodka would turn into an effective secret weapon. No sooner had the Russians reached the dump than the fighting spirit of the regiments evaporated for the time being. It took them three days to empty all those carboys of vodka …' Corporal Otto Tenning of 2nd Company, 3rd Grenadier Regiment, wrote in his diary: 'While the comrades on the other

side were sleeping off their vodka hangovers and forgetting all about this accursed war, the newly brought up *SS-Wiking* Panzer Division used the time for digging in undisturbed on the high ground behind Feski.'

DNIEPER RETREAT

It was a mere interlude. By 12 August, in an area of hills northwest of Kharkov, a powerful enemy force, whose manpower greatly exceeded that of *Wiking*, rammed into the division that had sped to the area behind *Totenkopf* and *Das Reich*. *Wiking* held its own for the next six days until the Russians, in a characteristic foray before a major engagement, teased out the front with their battalions and tank support. Two Soviet tank corps were beaten off, but in view of the overall situation, it was scant consolation. The beleaguered 3rd Panzer Division was forced to retreat in the face of opposition; *Grossdeutschland* and *Das Reich* sped to fill the gaps, but by then it was too late. Kharkov, south of Belgorod, and held by Army Detachment *Kempf, Das Reich* and *Totenkopf*, was to prove an impossible position to maintain. Hitler's predictable order to hold the city at all costs looked like having some merit for a while

Below: Street-fighting during the recapture of Kharkov. After his death, Stalin was blamed for the city's original loss, having issued 'no retreat' orders which caused the needless surrender of thousands of men.

when the Russians were thrown back at first. However, a three-pronged threat by Russian tanks made the end inevitable. The Fifth Tank Army of General Pavel Rotmistrov was hurled at General Erhard Raus's II Corps. The latter were the city's main defenders but there was no prospect of holding Kharkov. To escape encirclement and amid fresh fury from Hitler, the city was evacuated on 22 August. Later in the month the steady advance of Soviet forces meant withdrawal by the *Waffen-SS* to the River Dnieper. The list of key sectors rolled up by the Russians grew. Smolensk was recaptured by Marshal Sokolovsky of the Soviet Western Front. There was steamroller advance on Kiev and by 2 October the Germans had been driven a distance of 240km (149 miles) westward. A crossing of the Dnieper was forced, providing yet another example of Hitler's penchant for delayed withdrawal when no alternative existed. When the retreat from the Dnieper came, it proved a nightmare. With no time to prepare

Above: Counting the cost. When the land in which these graves were dug was recaptured by the Soviets, these makeshift crosses were desecrated or removed to prevent any permanent memorials to *Waffen-SS* dead.

roads, river crossings, demolition charges or minefields, Manstein, commander of Army Group South, had to conduct a withdrawal in the face of the Red Army whilst rowing with Hitler over the necessity of retreat.

SOVIET PRESSURE

The Russians scrambled to outflank the retreating Germans. Towards the end of September, fighting centred opposite Kanev, south of which the forces of

Right: After the Germans' failure at Kursk, the Soviets turned to the offensive. The biggest disaster for the Germans was the loss of Kharkov on 23 August, followed later by the Soviet crossing of the Dnieper.

BELORUSSIA

Smolensk, 25 Sept

Mogilev

Bryansk Front (Popov)

Army Group Centre (Kluge)

Bryansk

Orel, 5 Aug

Gomel

Central Front (Rokossovsky)

Kursk

U S S R

Voronezh Front (Vatutin)

Prokhorovka

Lyutezh

Belgorod, 5 Aug

Steppe Front (Koniev)

Kiev, 6 Nov

Army Group South (Manstein)

Bukrin

Soviet parachute drop, 26-27 Sept

Kanev

Kharkov, 23 Aug

Balakleya

Southwest Front (Malinovsky)

Izyum

Donets

UKRAINE

Cherkasskoye

Slavyansk

South Front (Tolbukhin)

Dnepropetrovsk

Bug

Hydro-electric dam

Zaporozhye

Army Group A (Kleist)

Mius

Taganrog

Red Army reaches mouth of the Dnieper, Dec 1943

Melitopol

Odessa

Kherson

German Seventeenth Army cut off in the Crimea, Dec 1943

Black Sea

Sea of Azov

Legend:
- Soviet advances
- East Wall – German defensive line
- Front line, 12 July 1943
- Front line, 4 Nov 1943

Dnieper

Desna

General Nicolai Vatutin's Voronezh Front had narrowed, breasting the Dnieper. Caught in the conflict around this time was *SS-Standartenoberjunker* Jan Munk of *Westland*. Professorial in manner and bespectacled, Munk hardly conformed to Himmler's ideal of pure Aryan manhood. Nevertheless, the young Dutchman was an eager volunteer with *Westland*:

'The barrage was very close by. I heard one gun in particular whose rounds landed short and to our left, then the next one was to our left but nearer still. The one following was a bull's eye. It landed right in front of us and destroyed our machine gun. We had been a split-second too late in taking cover. It felt as if an enormous weight had pushed me violently down. My number two started to splutter that the bastards had blown his nose off. It wasn't quite that bad, though. A tiny splinter had pierced his nose from one side right to the other, and he was bleeding like a stuck pig. We decided to go back to the bunker so that I could bandage him properly.

To my surprise I found that I couldn't move. I thought I had merely cut off the blood supply to my legs by squatting on my haunches. When the next shell came I was pushed, or so I thought, through the trench so fast that I could not keep upright, and I scraped my

Below: Men of the *Narva* battalion of the *Waffen-SS* are emulating the Red Army by riding on a captured T-34 into battle. Later T-34s had hand-holds welded onto their turrets to make it easier for infantry to hold on.

face on the ground. I shouted to my comrade not to be so bloody stupid and to calm down. He helped me to the bunker. Once inside, however, he told me that he hadn't touched me, let alone pushed me. It dawned on me that something wasn't quite right. My legs were still useless, so I undid my belt and the lower buttons of my tunic and tried to feel along my back, finding nothing, I loosened my trousers, and inspected that area. Still nothing. I dressed again and went back to bandaging my friend. We both had a smoke and then I began to feel hot and sweaty. I took my cap off and blood poured down over my face. With my fingers I could feel where the blood was coming from, a small cut right on the top of my head. Now I knew why my legs wouldn't work.

After a while I was carried through the trenches to an area where it was wide enough to use a stretcher. I was then brought to a collection point to wait for proper transport. Quite a few of our men were there, some on stretchers, some badly injured, some not so bad.

Above: In October 1943, *Waffen-SS* troopers stretcher a wounded comrade to safety. October was particularly traumatic for the Germans, with the Soviets digging in on the Dnieper, while Axis forces were stuck in the Crimea.

Then the Russians attacked again, and all the wounded who could walk were told to man their positions again. Those of us remaining were left behind to fend for ourselves as best we could. We were given some grenades and machine pistols and wished "good luck". We fully understood. More than a dozen men would have been needed to carry us away, and they couldn't be spared.

The Russians appeared and shot at us – we shot back. They threw hand grenades and we replied. Fortunately, the *Wehrmacht* counterattacked with the support of some light tanks. We did not lose a single wounded man, although some of us, including me, collected a few more wounds, though nothing serious. I was then taken by stretcher again to a *Wehrmacht* bunker.'

Between the Donetz and the Dnieper, fighting had been unrelenting for an entire week, with fatigue eating away at the effectiveness of the Germans. *Westland* suffered a severe blow when its leader, *Obersturmführer* (Lieutenant) Dieckmann, was killed in action on the central Dnieper, fighting for what had been dubbed *Fuchsschwanz* (Foxtail) Island, where a heavy bridgehead had been established and an attack mounted by *Westland's* amphibious tanks. A hardy veteran of the regiment, Dieckmann did not live to receive the Oak Leaves with Swords to his Knight's Cross.

With the generally continued deterioration of Germany's fortunes on the Eastern Front, Hitler's dependence on his SS cohorts became ever stronger.

Left: Leon Degrelle, the most celebrated non-German to serve with *Wiking*, made up for a lack of military experience with considerable physical courage. His unit never fully recovered from its ordeal in the Cherkassy pocket.

Above: A camouflaged *Wiking* PzKpfw IV tank on the Eastern Front, pictured in November 1943 during an medal awards ceremony. Broadly speaking, SS vehicle camouflage duplicated that of the *Wehrmacht*.

The need to reinforce his manpower was hastened by the withdrawal of the Finns. Their leader, Marshal Baron Mannerheim, had long lost any faith in the Germans since Hitler's failure to capture Moscow, thus putting ultimate victory in doubt. By August 1944, Mannerheim had become determined to take the country out of the war with the Soviet Union which had cost Finland 50,000 lives. To balance the loss of the Finns, there came a welcome reinforcement for *Wiking*, provided by collaborating Belgians. To Hitler, the man who could best achieve his 'European ideal' in Belgium was Leon Degrelle of the Walloons. The former religious publisher turned politician had become absorbed early on with the rise of fascism in

Above: A flak unit of SS-Panzer-Division *Wiking* manning a 20mm (0.78in) four-barrelled *Flakvierling* (antiaircraft gun) designed to engage low-flying enemy aircraft. As the war progressed, they were also used against ground targets.

Europe. Far from deaf to the hoarse demagogy of the German and Italian dictators with their mass meetings and parades, bands and banners, Degrelle had wanted a party of his own. The result had been the birth of the Christus Rex movement in 1935.

In Belgium however, Germany had encountered considerable difficulties in recruiting volunteers because of the presence of two separate ethnic groups. These were the Flemings, more racially akin to the Dutch, and the French-speaking Walloons, who regarded the Flemings as 'beyond the pale'. At first, only the 'racially pure' Flemings were permitted to join Himmler's cohorts, with the Walloons consigned to the *Wehrmacht* where selection was less rigid. Ultimately,

though it was the Walloons who provided a useful pool of recruits for the *Waffen-SS*. They were never less than enthusiastic; within a short time of formation they had attracted a strength of 1200 volunteers.

DEGRELLE'S DISASTER

Degrelle, a man lacking in military experience but possessing considerable charisma and physical courage, had insisted on offering himself as a front-line soldier. It was not his first attempt to don uniform. Before the start of 'Operation Barbarossa', he had asked to serve in the *Wehrmacht* but had been turned down on the grounds that he was 'indispensable to your political work'. At the time of the invasion of the Soviet Union he tried again, and this time there was no objection. He turned down the offer of a commission, arguing that he knew nothing of command and preferred to start in the ranks. At this time the infant Walloon unit was simply Infantry Battalion No 373, then the *Franc*

Wallonien Corps, fighting at the opposite end of the line from its compatriots in the Flemish Legion. The men were decked out in the standard army uniform with the addition, on the left upper arm, of a shield in the Belgian national colours surmounted by the word '*Wallonien*' in white. Action on the Don Front opposite Stalingrad was followed by the general switch to the Caucasus, where the cost in manpower was disastrous and Degrelle himself was one of the 850 wounded. Although he lacked military experience, there was, however, general agreement that he possessed considerable soldierly ability, marked by a succession of awards: the Knight's Cross of the Iron Cross, followed by the honour of Knight's Cross with Oak Leaves. It was a singular distinction for a non-German. The Walloons were admitted into the charmed circle of the *Waffen-SS* in June 1943 when the unit had reached a strength of 1600; constant pleading by Degrelle himself had paid off. With the designation of SS Volunteer Assault Brigade and well-equipped, *Wallonien* started out on its march to join *Wiking* at Korsun, well beyond the Dnieper, where a 96km (60-mile) deep salient divided

the two Soviet Army Groups of General Nicolai Vatutin and General (later Marshal) Ivan Koniev.

BLEAK PROSPECTS

Hitler's intention was to hold onto the salient with six-and-a-half divisions of around 56,000 troops. He would then thrust forward to Kiev some 64km (40 miles) away and restore a defensive line on the Dnieper. General Koniev's 2nd Ukrainian Front punched through the bridgehead lying between Kremenchug, which lay far to the southwest of Kharkov and Dnepropetrovsk to the east of Kremenchug. Koniev's objective was to form a wedge between First Panzer Army and Eighth Army. The latter was no match for the strong Soviet muscle and was forced to pull back in the face of the steady advance of the 2nd Ukrainian Front. In the north, things were no better, with ever more powerful Russian

Below: As the Soviet offensive gained momentum in late 1943, there was much hard fighting for the *Waffen-SS*. Note the stick grenades in the belt of the trooper on the left, placed there for easy access.

Above: Belgian *Waffen-SS* volunteers, most of whom were Walloons from Leon Degrelle's Rexist movement. Assigned to the *Waffen-SS* in June 1943, they later became the 28th SS Volunteer Panzergrenadier Division.

forces throwing the Germans out of Kiev on 6 November after they had established a bridgehead there. Russian pride was further restored with the recapture, after a temporary loss, of the town of Zhitomir on 20 November. Buildings there were reduced to rubble and the streets were littered with the burnt-out hulks of vehicles. Of considerable compensation were the large supply dumps and foodstuff depots of Fourth Panzer Army which the Germans had established in the high summer of triumph two years before. The men of *Wallonien* faced an unfamiliar adversary: Russian partisan bands, extremely competent with their light machine guns and automatic rifles. As bands of highly professional men, they were more

than capable of taking the place of regular Soviet infantry who could be freed for more pressing duties. But for all the efforts of the Panzer units and the SS, the truth was that the Soviet advance had become a flood with the great winter offensive dealing the decisive blow. Not the least disastrous was the overwhelming of Army Group Centre when, in mid-December, the Soviets burst out of the salient at Nevel in their progress southwest. Another knockout blow was delivered the following month by the Red Army in the north, forcing Army Group North to give up its encirclement of Leningrad.

SOVIET PRESSURE

Koniev's intention was to secure the vital West Ukrainian industrial city of Kirovograd, ahead of which lay the river Bug, nestling up to the Romanian border. Hitler's wish was to thrust forward from there to Kiev, some 64km (40 miles) away, and restore a defensive

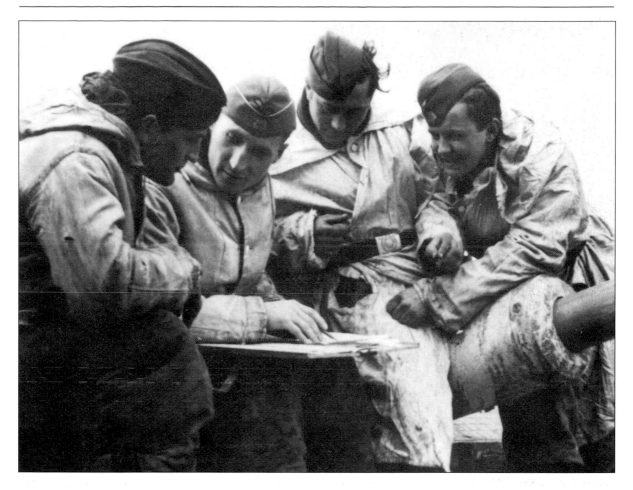

line on the Dnieper. The men of *Wiking* and *Wallonien* were assigned to territory where the prospects were bleak for the Germans. Four of their eleven divisions were encircled in this flat countryside under snow with the temperature in Kirovograd itself at minus 20 degrees Centigrade. On 5 January, Koniev's 2nd Ukrainian Front launched its attack and took the city. A breakout was eventually achieved by 3rd Panzer Division with fire cover from the artillery; engineers and panzergrenadiers followed, while the Russians were pinned down in local fighting. The conquest of Kirovograd still left unfinished business for the Russians. To the north lay the salient around Korsun and Cherkassy which Hitler was determined to hold and which was defended by six-and-a-half divisions with around 56,000 men. Manstein wanted to open the

Above: Time snatched for a map conference on the Eastern Front. By 1944 the *Waffen-SS* were facing a seemingly unstoppable Red Army, and Himmler's precious divisions were used to plug gaps in the line.

pocket, but Hitler insisted contact must be established with the beleaguered forces: the Dnieper line would be held, no matter the cost. The German positions south of the Korsun bulge took the full bombardment. Fourth Guards and Fifty-Third Armies, soon followed by Fifth Tank Army, struck at the heart of the German line. From the north of the bulge came 1st Ukrainian Front with its massive armour. By 28 January it had joined Koniev's 2nd Ukrainian Front, which had advanced from the south. Men of 5th SS-Panzer-Division *Wiking* were among the 60,000 trapped there.

CHAPTER SIX

ENCIRCLEMENT

The steamroller advance of the Red Army achieved the encirclement of 75,000 German troops in the Korsun salient, a breakout only gained at vast cost. Then came the strong defence by the Russians of Kovel, the springboard to the thrust of their forces across the river Bug.

Korsun was encircled from the north and south. Matters for the Germans could scarcely be worse. The frozen land between the Dnieper and the Bug hosted the powerful blizzards which sliced through the Ukraine's midwinter, where temperatures plunged to minus 15 degrees Centigrade and the snow piled 1m (3ft) thick. Within the pocket, 1st Panzer Division did what it could to bolster the weakened subunits of the 198th Infantry. Combat groups were reached by supply columns edging through the snow. The eventual arrival of warm winds signalled the thaw and the advent of *'rasputitsa'* – glutinous mud that clamped on men's boots and sucked them off the feet which were already stricken with frostbite. Vehicles had their tracks clogged or ripped off. Tanks and assault guns of *Wiking* somehow fought their way through the mess but the distances covered were pathetic: 3–4km (2–2.5 miles) in a single hour, the vehicles' fuel gauges nosediving. In the centre of the pocket lay the village of Korsun, around which the battle raged. Hitler, the ultimate map general, safe in his command centre, was incapable of looking beyond his charts of the streaking

Left: A shared loaf of bread for these SS *panzergrenadiers* in a rare fighting lull, while one of their number stands guard with stick grenades on the lip of the trench, ready for use.

arrows signifying an advance. He would tolerate no breakout for those trapped within the bulge. Rather, his forces would break into it. Then would come the ultimate trouncing of the encircling Soviet divisions. The advance would go on and Kiev would be won back. An order was given to the trapped corps commanders to stand fast in their positions, which encompassed 320km (200 miles), and screen off their rear with a new front. Six battered divisions would bear the brunt. Among many in the German general staff, it all seemed eerily like a rerun of Stalingrad. Memories of that humiliation, where attempts at relief had been 'too little, too late', haunted Manstein particularly.

RESCUE OPERATION

The task force's rescue operation to smash through into the pocket was launched on 4 February 1944. Assigned to the task was Lieutenant-General Hans Valentin Hube. One of the most experienced panzer leaders in the German Army, he was a man of few words. A laconic radio-telegraph message reached the beleaguered outpost: 'I'm coming.' Hube kept his promise, with III Panzer Corps boring a hole in the outer Russian defences in a push to Lysyanka which lay south of Korsun. Meanwhile, the weather had steadily deteriorated. Thaw had followed the snow; wet roads softened under the weight of incessant, heavy traffic.

Every shelter and trench was flooded; men were tasked to bail them out with pitchers and mess tins. The psychological advantage of the Russians over those trapped within the pocket was swiftly exploited. Leaflets targeted at *Wiking* and *Wallonien* were dropped by air, proclaiming the inevitability of an ultimate Soviet victory. One prisoner of the Russians, General von Seydlitz-Kurzbach who had been captured at Stalingrad, had a letter sent to *Gruppenführer* (Lieutenant-General) Gille, pleading on behalf of fellow captives, who were members of the self-proclaimed 'Alliance of German Officers', for the surrender of those trapped in the pocket. Seydlitz was despatched to the front line to address the troops with a loud hailer. In his account, Peter Strassner wrote: 'They certainly made no impression on the men of the *Waffen-SS.*'

Left: A surprise is prepared for a Soviet tank. By detaching the heads of several stick grenades and wrapping them around another grenade, a potent antitank weapon could be improvised, if the user could get close enough.

Above: Some 75,000 Germans were trapped in the pocket near Korsun and Cherkassy. These are just some of the 35,000 who managed to achieve a breakout after refusing a surrender ultimatum.

MAKESHIFT REFUGE

The Russians, however, did have some anxieties about the strength of the forces inside the pocket, even going to the extent of sending reconnaissance patrols in enemy uniforms to penetrate the fronts and quiz unsuspecting guards on the strength of units and weaponry. At this point it was still possible for the Junkers transport aircraft to home in on the airstrip near Korsun. Each day some 70 or so aircraft arrived, loaded with munitions, petrol and food. Once unloaded, they were filled with the seriously wounded for evacuation. But the Junkers were lumbering, slow transport planes and easy targets. Leon Degrelle wrote the Russians 'would patrol the drizzling sky, circling like hawks above the field. Every day, 12 of 15 of our *Jus* [Junkers transports], shot down after a few minutes of flight, would fall down in flames amid the screams of the wounded, who were being grilled alive …' When landing was no longer possible because of the rain inundating the landing field, the casualties were afforded refuge in makeshift buildings.

HOUSE-TO-HOUSE

In the early days, *Wallonien* escaped the worst of the enemy's clawing since the Russians were concentrating their thrust south and west of the pocket. But the Belgians had other troubles. An entire platoon of around 50 Russian auxiliaries had previously been absorbed into their ranks. These were prisoners who, in exchange for their lives, had been allowed to enlist in the German Army. Now these men were sensing the way the war was going and also had certain knowledge of what would happen to them if they did not return to their former allegiance. With the help of partisans, the renegade Russians began slipping out of the Walloon lines, having first disposed of their Belgian guards with a swift knife thrust. Any breathing space which might have been created for the Walloons was soon over.

The Soviet advance deepened. There was a request for more tanks, but only two could be mustered. They pressed deep into the Soviet advance, columns of Belgians bunched tightly behind. Degrelle recorded: 'On the plain, the Soviets rolled in like a flood tide, pulling along their light artillery. They spotted our two Panzers moving along the bare hillside. Immediately, an avalanche of shells rained down from their antitank weapons, boxing in our tanks, cutting off the top of the ramparts, killing our men.' The Belgians cleared the village of Staroselye where a neighbouring hill was dominated by a windmill with its motionless white sails, a vantage point for machine-gun nests whose snipers tracked every move. Leon Degrelle's driver, Leopold Van Doele, rushed ahead of the tanks, emptying his submachine gun into three Russians sheltering behind the windmill, before being struck down. By 16:00 hours, the hill had been taken. Degrelle wrote bitterly: 'We had taken quite a haul of machine guns, but what did we have more than yesterday? Nothing. In fact, we had lost a number of our comrades. Killing the Soviets didn't do any good. They multiplied like woodlice.'

Right: This radio post is manned by volunteers from the Flemish area of Belgium serving with the *SS-Westland* regiment, part of the *Wiking* Division. The regiment was involved in the breakout from the Korsun pocket.

Resistance was kept up against a succession of Soviet attacks from villages inside the ever-shrinking pocket. One of these villages, Shenderovka, which had previously fallen to the *Germania* Regiment, was chosen for what was seen as a pivotal role by Eighth Army, in overall command of the pocket. General Wilhelm Stemmermann, one of the German commanders, received an order to 'shorten the front lines and move the pocket in the direction of Shenderovka in order to be able, when the time comes, to breakout towards the forces mounting a relief attack from the outside.' The Russians in the meantime had delivered a major blow by retaking Komarovka, the southern anchor of the breakout front. For Stemmermann this meant revising his plans drastically since the loss endangered both the southern flank and the units which, it was planned, would follow the first assault waves. At Dzhurzhentsy, which was on high ground, it had been intended to place tanks. But it was possible to deploy only three tanks, and it was not long before heavy fire from the flanks forced them back behind the hill. Hospital trains were being brought up by First Panzer Army to the closest station behind the front; Junker 52s stood by to take on the wounded from Uman airfield.

On the planned line of departure from the pocket, Stemmermann stationed his corps detachments on north and centre positions, while *Wiking* was in the south. Conditions were such that although the detachments consisted of several divisions, they were greatly reduced in strength and overall were equivalent to one standard infantry division. A significant threat was a clutch of dwellings held by the Russians in the village of Novaya-Buda, lying to the south. Here they showed one of their greatest strengths: sustained training in effective house-to-house fighting. Red Army soldiers would melt away, then suddenly reappear in a score of places. Trees that had been scoured minutes before and found harmless would conceal snipers. *SS-Obersturmbannführer* (Lieutenant-Colonel) Lucien

Lippert, *Wallonien's* commander, led an attack on one of the dwellings. A momentary pause in a doorway proved fatal. Lippert took a bullet straight to his stomach. The men of *Wallonien* were determined not to let the body of their comrade fall into enemy hands. One Belgian, his arm shot through, rushed the enemy and crawled along with his fellows to secure the corpse which was then strapped between two boards and carried like a stretcher. However, Novaya-Buda was not abandoned before *SS-Sturmbannführer* (Major) Schumacher had destroyed 10 T-34s. This and other feats earned him promotion to *SS-Obersturmbannführer* and the award of the Knight's Cross.

TEMPORARY CORRIDOR

At Shenderovka, those attempting to break through into the pocket had fared worse. To widen the gap had proved impossible; by now vehicles were barely able to move and the village had become a repository for some 4000 wounded. A successful counterattack by a small *Wiking* panzer group proved a false dawn. The rollercoaster advance of the Red Army was unstoppable and the village was snatched from German hands in less than an hour, and the advancing panzer troops quickly died to a man.

Shenderovka, too, was the scene of the evacuation of some of the worst of *Wiking's* wounded. Their stretchers had been loaded aboard tracked vehicles. When these were no longer available in sufficient numbers, the casualties from the dressing station were loaded onto crude peasant carts, many of which were carrying Red Cross flags. This made no difference to the Russians; tanks and carts alike were torched by some 15 T-34s. West of Shenderovka, other vehicles of the Medical Company of *Wiking* came under attack and there were a bare dozen survivors. For the remnants, movement now could only be on foot along glutinous, muddy roads, where any vehicles which were still serviceable had to be abandoned.

Left: This Norwegian NCO of *Wiking* is clearly grateful for the latest supply of winter clothing which reached the men trapped in the Korsun and Cherkassy pocket, dropped from *Luftwaffe* Junkers Ju 52 aircraft.

Above: Field Marshal Erich von Manstein – suitably protected in his fur-lined coat against the hostile cold of winter – congratulates some of those fortunate to escape from the Korsun pocket.

Manstein by now realized only too well that hope for more mobile reserves was plain illusion. The Russians would not give up the encirclement battles which by now were proving impossible to oppose effectively. The solution was to get out of the Dnieper bend for good and retreat at least as far as the line of the Ukrainian Bug. With literally the last of his panzers, a temporary corridor was driven through to the encircled men in the Korsun-Shevchenkovski area of the lower Dnieper, where *Wiking* and the remnants of seven other divisions were entrapped. Hitler, at first deaf to the pleadings from Manstein, finally consented to a breakout. A brave but fruitless foray was made when, in a snowstorm, Stemmermann gathered some

Right: Leon Degrelle seen with his *Wallonien* survivors after the siege of the Korsun pocket in January–February 1944, which had resulted in heavy casualties for the Belgian *Waffen-SS*. Only 632 of Degrelle's men survived.

of his men, and crept out and slit the throats of the Soviet sentries. The next move was to assemble what transport there was and make for Lsyanka, where there was the possibility of a link-up with III Panzer Corps. Major Kampov, an officer on Koniev's staff, told the journalist Alexander Werth how the German forces:

'... had almost no tanks left – they had all been lost and abandoned during the previous days' fighting and what few tanks they still had now had no petrol. In the last few days the area where they were concentrated was so small that transport planes could no longer bring them anything. Even before, few of the transport planes reached them, and sometimes the cargoes of food and petrol and munitions were dropped on our lines.

So that morning they formed themselves into two marching columns of about 14,000 each, and they marched in this way to Lysanka ... beyond our front line, inside the "corridor". The German divisions on the other side were trying to batter their way eastward, but now the "corridor" was so wide that they hadn't much chance.

They were a strange sight, these two German columns that tried to break out. Each of them was like an enormous mob. The spearhead and the flanks were formed by the SS men of the *Wallonien* Brigade and the *Wiking* Divisions in their pearl-grey uniforms. They were in a relatively good state of physique. Then, inside the triangle marched the rabble of the ordinary German infantry, very much more down-at-heel. Right in the middle of this, a small select nucleus was formed by the officers. They also looked relatively well fed. So they moved westward along two parallel ravines. They had started out soon after 4 am, while it was still completely dark.

The Russians knew the direction from which the officers were coming. Five lines had been prepared – two of infantry, then a line of artillery, and then two more lines where the tanks and cavalry lay in wait.

We let them pass through the first three lines without firing a shot. The Germans, believing they had dodged us and had now broken through all our defences, burst into frantic jubilant screaming, firing their pistols and tommy-guns into the air as they marched on. They had now emerged from the ravines and reached open country.'

NO PRISONERS

Around 06:00 hours, Russian cavalry and tanks charged into the thick of the two columns. It was a massacre that extended over four hours. The tanks chased the scattering Germans without mercy, crushing them as they ran in terror through the ravines. Gunfire was kept to the minimum, lest the closely bunched tanks hit one another. There was no time or inclination to take prisoners. When it was over, 20,000 Germans had been killed. Leon Degrelle was also a witness to these events and he vividly recalled the frantic bids which were made to quit the pocket:

'Vehicles were overturned, throwing wounded in confusion to the ground. A wave of Soviet tanks overtook the first vehicles and caught more than half the convoy; the wave advanced through the carts, breaking them under our eyes, one by one like boxes of matches, crushing the wounded and the dying horses … We had a moment's respite when the tanks got jammed in the procession, and were trying to get clear of the tangle of hundreds of vehicles beneath their tracks.'

The dressing stations could accept no more men; each unit was made responsible for evacuating its own. In one instance, a 183kg (18-ton) tractor with three machine-gun crews drove behind the combat forces as protection for the wounded. Among them was SS-*Standartenoberjunker* Raymond Lemaire, who in pre-SS days had joined the Walloon Legion of the *Wehrmacht*. After hard training in Dresden he had returned to the unit in October 1943 as a member of *Wallonien* and had moved up to the front at Cherkassy:

Left: These men emerged from the chaos of the breakout from the Korsun pocket to reach the German lines. Survivors from *Wiking* had to be withdrawn from the front line after the evacuation for refitting.

'We pioneers had to occupy some of the infantry positions to maintain the line. After numerous actions and battles, I was the only NCO left in my platoon!

The Soviets attacked our sector on 30 January, but in two hours of hand-to-hand and close-quarter fighting we managed to beat them off. However, I was seriously wounded by grenade splinters in both legs in the process. Being unable to walk, after a few hours I was evacuated by plane out of the pocket. I subsequently spent eight weeks in hospital, following which I received three weeks leave. My unit managed to escape from the encirclement, but in all 700 men out

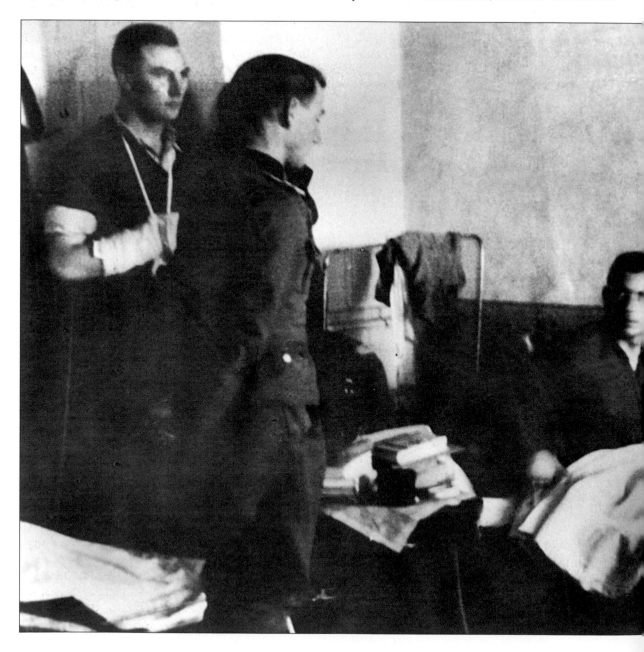

of a total of 2000 Walloons died in the period from the end of November 1943 to 17 February 1944.'

SWEPT AWAY

Taken up in the retreat also were the men of *Germania*, under *SS-Obersturmbannführer* (Lieutenant-Colonel)

Fritz Ehrath. A report subsequently revealed: 'Using only close-combat weapons, the brave Grenadiers of *Germania* destroyed 24 Soviet tanks and in bitter close-quarters fighting prevented the splitting of the pocket.' One key point where the fast-moving Soviet tanks moved in for the kill, crushing those who had not fallen to the guns, was the Gniloy Tikich River, the crossing of which was vital for the escaping Germans so that they could reach the safe haven of Lsyanka. It turned out to be a perilous venture for *Wiking* which came up against heavy machine-gun fire. On arrival at the river there was no time to register that the temperature was five degrees below centigrade, particularly when four T-34s opened up with high explosive shells and ricocheting air bursts. There were those who lost their heads and jumped blindly into the icy waters, where there was no hope of survival.

Once the firing had eased, all attention was on the rugged figure who stood by the river bank, imperturbable in his fur jacket and sporting a knobbly stick. As calmly as if he was conducting an exercise, *Obergruppenführer* (General) Gille, the *Wiking* Commander, had managed to get about 4500 men of *Wiking* Division safely to this spot and had no intention of losing them now. Of this he was particularly determined, for in repulsing murderous and repeated tank attacks they had suffered the heaviest casualties of the entire breakout. Gille ordered the last tractor to be driven into the river to become a makeshift pier for an emergency footbridge, only to see it swept away by the current. Farm carts fared no better. His next move was to sort out the swimmers and non-swimmers into human chains, alternating with one swimmer with one non-swimmer. Gille himself stepped into the water at the head of the first chain which unfortunately broke half way across, ending the lives of the non-swimmers. The second attempt was no better and there were more men drowned. With the rearguard came *SS-Hauptsturmführer* Dorr of *Germania* whose men were

Left: *Obergruppenführer* **(General) Herbert Gille,** *Wiking* **commander, decorating the wounded after their escape. Universally respected within the division, Gille believed in sharing at first-hand all the dangers of battle.**

Left: Although there were numerous breakouts from the pocket, many Germans were taken prisoner. The future of these SS men was bleak. Few would ever see Germany again, imprisoned for life deep in the Soviet Union.

pulling the last survivors of the casualty transport through the snow and whose lot had been to look after the columns of wounded. It is worthy of note that along with them across the river went the body of Lucien Lippert wrapped in a sheet of tent canvas.

THE SURVIVORS RETURN

Under fire from the Soviet tanks, the first survivors across the Gniloy Tikich, streaming with icy water and often stark naked, ran through the snow to the distant cottages of Lysanka. Others, in uniforms frozen rock solid, staggered like zombies into the arms of pickets of the *Leibstandarte* and 1st Panzer Division. The full brunt of the Soviet assault and, therefore, the major casualties at Cherkassy were taken by *Wiking* and *Wallonien*. According to Degrelle, on arrival at the Dnieper in 1942, the strength of the Walloon force had stood at around 2000 men. On withdrawal from the pocket on 18 February 1944, the figure was 632. To add to everything, in their retreat from the pocket, the escapers had to suffer being riddled with countless biting crystals of ice, the product of gales and the swirling snowstorms. As they slowly progressed, they saw graphic evidence of the cost of the three-month battle. The men of *Wallonien* came across a graveyard of tanks: 800 Soviet and 300 German tanks had been destroyed. During the thaw, scores of Panzers had bogged down in the spongy earth, sinking into it over their treads. When the frost returned, the tanks were rooted to the spot. The remnants of *Wiking* had barely escaped with their lives, and that equipment which they could carry with them; this amounted to little beyond their haversacks and at most their light weapons.

On the second day of the retreat in the direction of Poland the icy grip relaxed and so, for a while, did the fury of the Soviet pursuit. The sun turned the snow pink and shining. But a further privation awaited the survivors. No sooner had they settled into makeshift accommodation than they learnt that leave would only be granted to 'the Germanic volunteers and the wounded'. The rest, including many who had been given leave by their officers, were ordered by Hitler to reassemble at Lublin. A change of heart, however, was brought about after Degrelle urged Hitler to exempt *Wallonien*, whose men were granted 21 days leave. At *Führer* headquarters Hitler presented *Obergruppenführer* (General) Gille with the Swords and Oak Leaves to the Knight's Cross of the Iron Cross, while *SS-Hauptsturmführer* (Captain) Degrelle received the Knight's Cross. Instructions from *Führer* Headquarters called for the rebuilding of the shattered forces of *Wiking* in the area of Lublin, where many of the survivors had ended up when they escaped the pocket.

The next key development in the war in the East was in the spring of 1944 when STAVKA, the Soviet High Command, decided to make Belorussia its priority in the north. It was Stalin's intention that the Red Army would drive from its starting point east of Lake Peipus, along a line running through Gorki in the centre, skirting the Pripet Marshes, and thus on to the Black Sea port of Odessa. It was hoped that the Germans, in the face of 19 armies and 2 tank armies, with some 1300 aircraft in support, would be slammed back some 650km (400 miles) to the very gates of Warsaw.

German attention now focused on Kovel, a key rail and road junction situated some 250km (160 miles) from Warsaw in the Pripet Marshes, east of the river Bug, and where it was considered vital to place a garrison. *Wiking* was given the task, but *Obergruppenführer* (General) Gille reported that his division could only muster small arms and was without heavy weapons or vehicles. Light machine guns and munitions were rushed from Warsaw. Trains were requisitioned to carry fresh forces of *Germania* and *Westland* to Kovel. On arrival Gille was greeted with alarming news. To the east of the city German forces had met with stiff opposition and had made a measured withdrawal. One of the expected trains carrying the men of *Germania* had been fired on by the Russians. The riposte with the meagre armoury of rifles and machine guns had proved fruitless and the train had to be abandoned. The contingents of *Westland* fared little better when their transport train was attacked and its occupants

Above: *Wiking* men and a Panther tank on the Eastern Front in May 1944 prepare to receive another Soviet attack. This may be a propaganda photograph, as they are extremely exposed to enemy air attack.

pinned down. A bid to advance into Kovel by *Germania* and *Westland* next day was set at naught by the strength of the enemy and it became clear that, until further relief forces materialized, virtually the only option was defence of the city from within; Kovel must now be turned into a fortified town.

SS-Hauptsturmführer (Captain) Westphal of *Wiking* related: 'As evening fell we gradually realized that we were sitting in a city which was slowly but surely being surrounded on all sides by enemy forces.' The presence of four Russian rifle divisions was reported. In the face of this opposition, mines and antitank obstructions were set up within the city with plans – when at all feasible – for an eventual breakout.

Left: A panzergrenadier fires a flare pistol into the air as a signal to other members of the Division. He carries a Kar 98K rifle in his left hand, and wears the camouflage smock unique to the *Waffen-SS*.

PANZER ATTACK

Called into action was the already proven expertise of *SS-Obersturmführer* (Lieutenant) Karl Nicolussi-Leck of *Wiking*'s 5th SS Panzer Regiment, a veteran of hard fighting as a panzer leader in the Caucasus and now heading a well-trained panzer company. There was the additional 'muscle' of 16 Panthers and the armoured battalion of *Germania* with additional infantry manpower. At 12:00 hours on 29 March, amid heavy snow-drifts, deployment began. Nicolussi-Leck recounted:

'Kovel was declared a "strongpoint", and I was given the task of striking through the Russian forces in the town and halting them while a counteroffensive could be launched to break through the encirclement. Because of the strong enemy forces and the snow-covered, swampy terrain, the breakthrough was very costly and time consuming. After ten hours of slow going in the face of resistance, as midnight approached, we had covered only half the distance, having lost a third of our armoured vehicles in the process. In this situation the breakthrough into the town began to appear hopeless. When my armoured spearhead was just 2km (1.5 miles) from Kovel, I received an order from my battalion commander to

halt. By this time, however, my lead tank was already in action against the enemy defenders in the northwest of the city. Knowing how desperate the situation had become, I disregarded the order and carried on with the attack.

Thanks to the cover afforded by a blizzard and severe snowdrifts that covered our left flank, after 18 hours of battle, and with only half of our army remaining, we reached the town in the early hours of the morning. We then defended the town against counter-attacks by superior enemy forces until an attack by a German panzer corps broke through the encirclement and the troops and wounded could be brought out. Throughout, the *Luftwaffe* had supplied us with rations, medicines, ammunition and petrol …

After fulfiling several requests in regards to combating enemy forces from units defending the northwest section of the city, I drove with several panzers to Gille's command post and reported to the *Gruppenführer* [General].'

STEEL ARMADA

The report included the destruction of tanks, antitank guns and rifles, mortars and light infantry weapons. An Order of the Day *(Tagesbefehl)* on 15 April stated:

'The *Führer* has awarded *SS-Obersturmführer* [Lieutenant] Nicolussi-Leck, commander of 8 Company, the Knight's Cross of the Iron Cross. Nicolussi-Leck, on his own initiative, and under difficult conditions, succeeded in breaking through to the encircled city of Kovel on 30 March 1944. His reinforcement of the garrison was decisive. He carries a special share in the credit for the city holding out.

In addition the Regiment is proud to know that such a deserving, long-serving member is being awarded this distinction. May soldier's good fortune stay with *SS-Obersturmführer* Karl Nicolussi-Leck.'

The achievement provided a fillip to the morale of the beleaguered fortress that Kovel had become. By

Left: A PzKpfw V Ausf G Panther of the *Wiking* Division in May 1944. The Panther was one of the latest German tanks and a match for the Soviet T-34. It was armed with a high-velocity 75mm (2.95in) gun.

way of orchestration and to stimulate fighting commitment still further, a German radio broadcast, addressed specifically to members of the Volunteer SS and monitored by the British listening stations, called for team spirit *(Mannschaft)*:

'Praise be to everything that makes us hard. Hard times call for hard hearts. Whenever the *Führer* talks to us he demands endurance and hardness from us … Never give up the struggle, never, even if everything appears hopeless! Fling the empty cartridge into the face of the enemy, take him with you if you have to die. Everyone must be able to march, to suffer hunger and thirst, to sleep on bare ground and endure all hardships with cheerful courage.'

In the event, it altered little. The Soviets, who had been hot on the heels of Nicolussi-Leck, once again sealed off Kovel from the west. By then, the Red Army was after infinitely bigger fish. While the struggle in

Above: A *Waffen-SS* MG34 machine-gun team take cover in a ditch. The gunner was always accompanied by a loader, who carried spare ammunition belts – 250 rounds in each box.

Normandy in the days following the D-Day invasion on 6 June 1944 was the preoccupation of the Allies in the West, muscles were being flexed for an attack by the Russians on the Eastern Front. The offensive was to be so vast that it involved some 160 divisions, more than 4000 tanks and self-propelled guns manned by 1.2 million troops, with additional support from 6000 Soviet aircraft. Codenamed 'Operation Bagration', after a Russian general who had fought against Napoleon, the object of the attack was for nine sectors to be made into fortified areas. These included Bobruysk on the Berezina, Mogilev and Orsha on the Dnieper, and Vitebsk on the Dvina.

DREAD OF SUMMER

As for the Germans at Kovel, they had, ironically, been viewing the approach of summer with something of the dread they normally reserved for the Russian winter. The marshes that were around the forests in the Kovel area had the effect of holding up the advance of tanks. But in the spring and beyond, the marshes began drying rapidly, obviously a big advantage for an attacking force. The assembly of Russian forces in the forests of the Kovel–Lublin rail line seemed a clear pointer to Russian intentions. The location would be a springboard to the crossings of the River Bug.

The Russians launched a massive tank offensive from east to west. The panzer crews encountered a dust-shrouded steel armada, previously held under cover, driving out the village of Maciejov under a massive coverage of fighter-bombers. One of the greatest strengths of the Germans at this point was their skilled use of camouflage. For a few vital minutes the advancing Russians were caught off guard. The situation was

assessed and exploited by *Obersturmführer* (Lieutenant) Olin, a Finn who had elected to stay with the *Waffen-SS* rather than return home when his country parted company with Germany. He drove into a camouflaged position with several Panthers and held his fire. Ten of the enemy's tanks were allowed to proceed unscathed, lulling the others into a false sense of security. Olin chose his moment. The duel lasted half an hour with the loss of 103 Soviet tanks. Other units harassed the progress of the Soviets who had been making for a rail bridge over the Bug. A total of 295 enemy tanks failed to make it. It was a small triumph, but even these were rarities for the Germans. For the victors of Maciejov, the drive was now further north; *Wiking's* task was to close with the Russians near Bialystok.

Below: New recruits for the *Waffen-SS* take the oath of loyalty to Adolf Hitler. After the loss of so many men in the Korsun pocket and elsewhere, the organization was forced to scour Europe for suitable replacements.

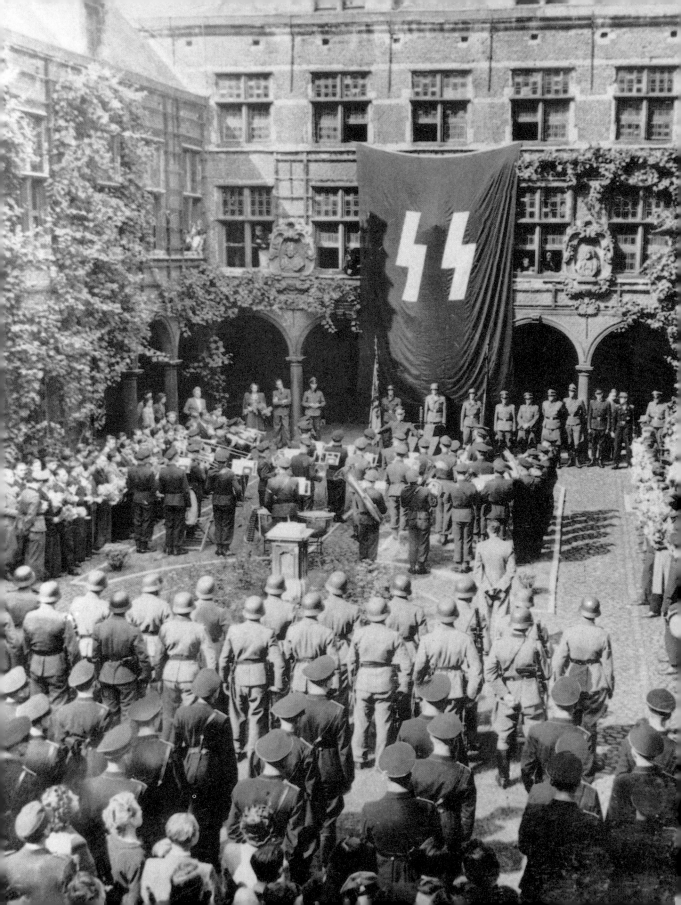

CHAPTER SEVEN

RETREAT

With his forces thrown out of Poland by the Red Army, Hitler made a fruitless bid to stand fast in Hungary, where the Soviets were able to hold Budapest in a vice. With dwindling manpower and material, the men of *Wiking* were forced back into the *Reich* itself.

After a brief period of training for fresh reservists, the newly (partly) equipped 5th SS-Panzer-Division *Wiking* made for Bialystok, northeast of Warsaw. The task was to blunt the steady advance of 2nd White Russian Front, the main burden of the battle falling at first on the men of *Westland*. Szyzowor was seized after a heavy opening bombardment, but after that point, the pattern was distressingly familiar. A counterattack was repelled but brought short-term relief. Russian manpower seemed to be inexhaustible; if one front sector held, then the enemy simply broke through to the left and right of it.

The greatest mass of forces was concentrated within Army Group Centre. Such a move was a recipe for disaster. Of the 38 divisions in the field, 28 were obliterated and 350,000 to 400,000 men were wounded, killed or missing. Vitebsk, regarded by Hitler as the most important of the fortified areas and which he vainly insisted on holding until the eleventh hour, was overrun; its destruction opened a breach in the German line more than 45km (28 miles) wide. As it turned out, the needs of Bialystok were put on hold, since the forces of

Germania and *Westland* had to be switched from one disaster area to another in the familiar 'fire brigade' role. Hopes were pinned on the 3rd SS-Panzer-Division *Totenkopf*, rushed by train to the Eastern Front from the Romanian theatre with the armoured Paratroop Division *Hermann Göring*. The intention was to secure the city of Siedlice, 80 km (50 miles) east of Warsaw.

NEW PANZER CORPS

The Russians seemed to hold the cards, but not all had been entirely well with the Red Army. It had received a jolt when, on the river Vistula's right bank, the Soviet Second Tank Army was beaten in battle just a few miles from Warsaw at a cost of 3000 killed and 6000 prisoners, together with the loss of a good deal of armour. Volume IV of the Soviet history, *The Great Patriotic War* contains some frank criticism of its forces:

'The tempo of the offensive had greatly slowed down. The German High Command had by this time thrown some very strong reserves against the main sectors of our advance. German resistance was strong and stubborn. It should also be remembered that our rifle divisions and tank corps had suffered heavy losses in previous battles; that the artillery and supply bases were lagging behind, and that the troops were short of both petrol and ammunition. Infantry and tanks were not receiving nearly enough artillery support ...'

Left: A ceremonial occasion at SS headquarters in Brussels on 30 July 1944. The city was liberated by the British on 3 September, and the supply of Belgian volunteers for the *Waffen-SS*, already dwindling, was cut off.

In a state of exhaustion, the forces of 1st Belorussian Front under Marshal Konstantin Rokossovsky faced the German bridgehead fronting Warsaw. Their lines of communication were stretched and men and materiel below strength. To exploit even these weaknesses in his enemy and to counter the defeat of Army Group 'North Ukraine' with its inevitable further grim consequences for Army Group Centre, Hitler proposed to strengthen his resources by harnessing the fighting prowess of *Totenkopf* with those of *Wiking*. The result, as decreed by Field Marshal Walther Model, was the creation of IV SS Panzer Corps, under the command of *SS-Obergruppenführer und General der Waffen-SS* (General) Herbert Gille. The corps was to include 3rd SS-Panzer-Division *Totenkopf* and 5th SS-Panzer-Division *Wiking*.

Gille was succeeded as *Wiking* commander first by *SS-Oberführer* (Senior Colonel) Edmund Deisenhofer, then by *SS-Standartenführer* (Colonel) Johannes Rudolf Muhlenkamp, who had been formerly attached to *Germania* during the Polish campaign, and finally by *SS-Standartenführer* Karl Ullrich.

ARMOUR BREAKTHROUGH

Instructions given to *Wiking* by IV SS Panzer Corps called for the division to edge back from the fighting to Brest-Litovsk (now Brest) on the Bug, followed by an immediate advance west to Warsaw. Its southern flank would then be screened against the pursuing enemy. A link there would be made with the *Totenkopf* which was assembling in the area of Siedlice as a component of IV

Below: After hurriedly camouflaging their position, these Estonian *Waffen-SS* troopers are consulting a map in the area of Narva, west of Leningrad. Narva was defended for months in the face of unrelenting Soviet pressure.

Right: This map illustrates the dramatic Soviet advance in the latter part of 1944 towards East Prussia, which was to lead to the encirclement and annihilation of 17 divisions of Hitler's Army Group Centre.

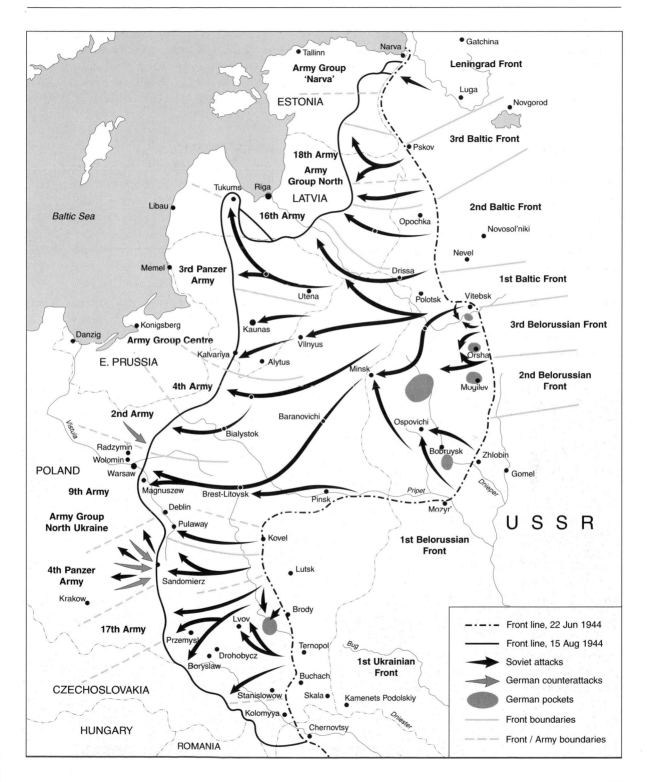

Baltic Sea

Tallinn
Narva
Gatchina

Army Group
'Narva'
Leningrad Front

ESTONIA
Luga
Novgorod

Pskov
3rd Baltic Front

18th Army
Army
Group North
LATVIA
2nd Baltic Front

Tukums
Riga
Opochka
Novosol'niki

Libau
16th Army
Nevel

Drissa
1st Baltic Front

Memel
3rd Panzer
Army
Polotsk
Vitebsk

Utena
3rd Belorussian Front

Konigsberg
Kaunas
Orsha

Danzig
Army Group Centre
Vilnyus
2nd Belorussian
Front

E. PRUSSIA
Kalvariya
Alytus
Minsk
Mogilev

4th Army
Baranovichi
Ospovichi

2nd Army
Bialystok
Bobruysk
Zhlobin

Vistula
Gomel

Radzymin
Wolomin
Warsaw
Brest-Litovsk
Pinsk
Pripet
Mozyr'
Dnieper

POLAND
9th Army
Magnuszew
Deblin
1st Belorussian
Front
USSR

Army Group
North Ukraine
Pulaway
Kovel

4th Panzer
Army
Lutsk

Krakow
Sandomierz
Brody

17th Army
Lvov
Ternopol
Bug

Przemysl
1st Ukrainian
Front

Drohobycz
Boryslaw
Buchach

CZECHOSLOVAKIA
Stanislowow
Skala
Kamenets Podolskiy

Kolomyya
Dniester

HUNGARY
Chernovtsy

ROMANIA

Front line, 22 Jun 1944
Front line, 15 Aug 1944
Soviet attacks
German counterattacks
German pockets
Front boundaries
Front / Army boundaries

SS Panzer Corps. A source of anxiety was the stream of enemy reinforcements assembling near the ancient town of Modlin which lay 30km (19 miles) north of Warsaw. The priority was to link up with other units assembled there and stem the tide. But nothing could stop the Russian spearheads driving on the heels of the German rearguards. Brest Litovsk was lost on 23 July.

At first, communication with *Totenkopf* created problems before it was able to join the rest of the strength situated in the bridgehead in the Warsaw suburb of Praga on a line from Brest-Litovsk. Eight days later, Soviet armour thrust into Otwock and Radzymin, bringing the Russians to within 19km (12 miles) of the Polish capital, northeast and east of Praga on the Vistula's eastern bank The area was a sheer fortress, a formidable array of pillboxes and fixed-firing positions, field fortifications, minefields, and strings of antitank and anti-infantry obstacles. Not only that but the Russians had stumbled into a vast concentration of German armour. In addition to *Wiking*, *Hermann Göring* and *Totenkopf* Divisions, there were two other panzer divisions, the 19th and the 4th. In trouble too

Above: In June 1944 Warsaw rose against the Germans before it could be liberated by the Soviet Union. Here members of the Polish 'Home Army' are blindfolded before being taken to discuss terms of surrender.

was the Soviet XI Tank Corps which, while trying to throw the Germans out of the region of Siedlice to the east, was dangerously low on fuel and ammunition. In addition, Second Tank Army, coming up against the latest German heavy tanks, 'Royal' or 'King' Tigers, was feeling the effect of considerable losses already sustained in the drive from Lublin.

In the area of Radzymin-Wolomin, northeast of Warsaw, the Russians fared better, pitching in with fighter-bomber assaults, the prelude to a bitter tank battle which caused *Westland* heavy casualties and forced the Division into a fighting withdrawal to the area of Malopole. By the end of August, there had been three vicious tank battles, with Malopole changing hands as many times. *Totenkopf* took the brunt of the action against an invigorated Soviet Eighth Army with 150-strong battery support. Nevertheless, the

Wiking Division was able to establish a north-south solid wedge running from the Bug to Malopole. A decision was taken to send out reconnaissance patrols as near as possible to the Russian lines. The patrols reported signs of movement by the Russians in the area of Czarnow, and within hours enemy tanks were on the move making for a key German bridgehead at a point on the Bug. An attempt was made to counterattack but the Panzers were unable to advance over the unsuitable terrain and the attack failed. The 12 panzers and assault guns (*Sturmgeschutzen* or StuGs) involved in the attack were blown up after being stripped of weapons and equipment in the ignominious retreat. The Germans then quit the bridgehead. Casualties on both sides were heavy. The Russians lost five Sherman-type tanks and T-34s; seven others were rendered useless.

This disaster was followed by a threat to an entire sector of the German corps, from the Vistula in the area of Zbytki to the Bug in the far north. In the early hours of 1 September the sector was covered by a heavy curtain of Russian fire that lasted a full hour. Resistance by the forces of *Westland* was puny, necessi-tating a series of withdrawals which allowed the Russians to establish another bridgehead at Pogozelec. Repeated attempts to reduce the bridgehead were to no avail, and it was enlarged when the Russian armour broke through from the north in the direction of Male. Here the familiar propaganda offensive was renewed with loud-speaker pleas to the *Waffen-SS* to surrender. Intelligence reached the division that the Russians were amassing 12–14 rifle divisions and other units for a drive through to the canal north of Praga. Their aim was to establish a bridgehead between Warsaw and the forests of Modlin. The interception of rations and other supplies parachuted into the area alerted the Germans to the presence of partisan bands lurking in the surrounding forests. The manpower situation of IV SS Panzer Corps was such that, for effective opposition to any attack, it would be necessary to depend upon yet

Below: An SS tank commander on the Eastern Front scans the horizon for potential targets. By this stage of the war, fuel was at a premium, and so commanders tried to eke out their limited supplies.

more reservists. But most were so green that additional training was required. This could only be carried out by withdrawing individual units from the front line, and they could not be spared. The Red Army had sprung northwards and captured Praga, which became the scene of intense street-fighting. The Russians, conscious of the strains suffered by their armour, had not committed themselves initially to a tank assault. Infantry came in first to reconnoitre and the price of their caution was an assault from the *SS-Totenkopf* Division, many of whom were gaunt and fatigued zombies who had held out for as long as possible.

'HOME ARMY' UPRISING

By then Warsaw was deep in its own very personal war; resistance fighters of the Polish 'Home Army' *(Armija Krajowa, AK)* began what was to be a 63-day struggle against the occupying German garrison. At first the Germans had withdrawn precipitately, but within days they returned, announcing to the citizens of Warsaw that the city would be defended and civilian labour conscripted to build fortifications. The Russians rolled into defensive positions and the infantry dug in. The men of AK forthwith launched their own offensive inside Warsaw, waging war on German installations and key points. The tragedy of the 'Warsaw Rising' ran its course until the capitulation of the 'Home Army' on 2 October. As accounts of the Warsaw rising make clear, the insurrection was put down with horrific brutality by SS freebooters, working with the notorious *Dirlewanger* and *Kaminski* brigades. No units of *Wiking* were involved. The Russians remained on the banks of the Vistula until the Germans had crushed the rebellion. According to accounts, this was on the orders of Stalin to whom the AK was anathema, regarded as 'power-seeking criminals' loyal to the Polish government-in-exile in London. A counter-argument pleaded that an advance by the Russians into Warsaw had not been an option, since by the time it faced the German

Left: Surrender to the Red Army was not an option open to the *Waffen-SS*: they were either shot out of hand or imprisoned in labour camps for life. Most tried to surrender to the Western Allies instead.

defences in front of Warsaw, the 1st Belorussian Front was in a state of exhaustion. A few days' respite had been necessary in order to receive major reinforcements in men and materiel.

CHANGE OF COMMAND

As far as *Wiking* was concerned, an important event on 9 October was a change in command for the Division when *SS-Standartenführer* (Colonel) Karl Ullrich, formerly a Pioneer Commander and Regimental Commander with the *Totenkopf* Division, succeeded *SS-Standartenführer* Johannes Rudolf Muhlenkamp. Ullrich's speedy arrival at Corps headquarters in a flurry of dust from an armoured personnel carrier *(Schutzenpanzerwagen)* had been dramatic. Radio intelligence had alerted the Germans to Russian plans for an attack on corps headquarters; the new commander and his staff huddled in the cellars. On the following day, the attack went ahead at Modlin, where Russian strength proved insufficient to envelop and destroy the SS divisions, and as a consequence the Soviets were obliged to call off their attack.

On the other hand, the infantry resources of *Wiking* were dwindling disastrously. Replacements garnered from the *Luftwaffe* proved to be more trouble than they were worth in the melee of ground warfare. The Russian tank riposte, when it came, involved T-34s and T-41s spread out over a 1km (1000yd) wide front. But infantry support for the tanks was negligible. The Russians gingerly worked their way along their lines of advance, hugging roadside ditches which were sometimes hidden from view. With his gun crews under rifle and machine-gun fire, *Oberscharführer* (Sergeant) Schmalz edged two flak guns towards the concealed ditches and other points of cover. It took just a few bursts to rout the enemy and force them into retreat. The road to Modlin was kept open.

At a point on the river Narew, the biggest tributary to the Vistula, the Division, which by then had been obliged to accept further raw recruits dropped by the *Luftwaffe*, was defending a position running south along a section of the river's 485km (303-mile) length. It soon became clear that these forays by the Russians heralded the renewed offensive on Warsaw itself.

Above: One of the thousands of non-combatant foreign volunteers with the *Waffen-SS*, seen early in the war. If captured by the Soviets, he would most likely be shot, or imprisoned for life in a labour camp if he was lucky.

Divisional troops became hard-pressed in the neighbourhood of the railway line at Lotnisko, where the Russians launched a two-hour barrage prior to their main attack. With their Sherman tanks, the Red Army forces plunged deep into the surrounding forest area. A steel curtain of artillery fire rendered any communication impossible, let alone access into the sector. Ambulances sent to pick up the growing numbers of wounded were either destroyed or beaten back. Men of the *Westland* Regiment were pinned down in the cemetery abutting the forest. An eventual breakthrough was made by a tough infantry contingent of 1st Battalion of 5th SS Panzer Regiment charged with winning back those sections of the rail line which had been lost. At the end of one evening, only 40 out of 400 men had survived, the wounded being crammed painfully into a single personnel carrier. The eventual appearance of panzers provided a breathing space during the breakout, although they had a tough time battling through the unfriendly forest terrain.

Around Warsaw itself, the Red Army had outrun its supply system and needed to gather strength before assaulting the German defences encircling the capital. The insurrection by the Polish 'Home Army' (AK) in Warsaw had cost 200,000 civilian and 15,000 AK lives. On 2 October the Poles capitulated. There were 10,000 dead among the 26,000 German casualties. With the Soviet offensive called to a halt, the Germans were able to crush the uprising. The surrender was signed by General Bor-Komorowski of AK. Warsaw was now almost completely destroyed.

The Red Army had, back in late August, been busy to the far south, and had brought about the capitulation of Romania, thus enabling the Russians to occupy

the key oilfields at Ploesti. The entire country was in Soviet hands by the end of the month. On 8 September the Soviet occupation of Bulgaria was underway. This month also marked the final exit from the war of the Finns, who for good measure turned on the German mountain troops who had refused to evacuate Finnish territory. Hitler's attention had, perforce, to be switched to western Europe where, back at the end of July, the Americans had launched their drive to smash out of the Normandy bridgehead. Alas, he could not afford to have his attention distracted. As well as the advancing Russians, there loomed the problem of Germany's erstwhile ally, Hungary. Hitler, ensconced in the *Adlerhorst*, the headquarters near

Below: A map showing German positions at the end of the war. *Wiking* was heavily involved in the defence of Budapest and Vienna. Many of the division who survived the war surrendered to the Americans.

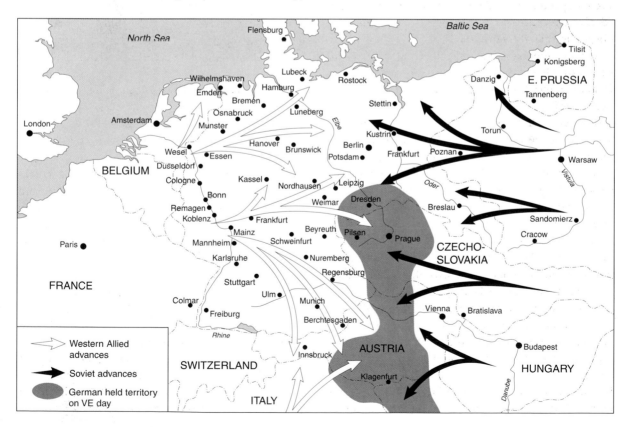

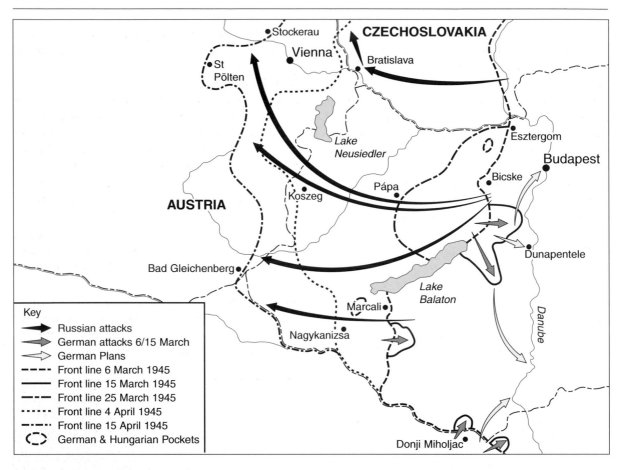

Berlin from which he commanded the Ardennes offensive, was showing further danger signs of being stuck in a Stalingrad-like time warp. As the vast Soviet wave of destruction rolled onwards towards Germany north of the Carpathians, Hitler found himself obsessed with Hungary. An attempt made in early October by Admiral Miklos Horthy, Hitler's puppet there, to defect to the Soviet side was quickly foiled by the Germans. Horthy was then pressed to continued subservience through the kidnapping of his playboy son, Nikolaus. The next move was to imprison the 76-year-old admiral and replace him with Ferenc Szalasi, a committed fascist. Meeting with Hitler, Szalasi agreed that the capital, Budapest, must be held 'at any price'. This was only possible if Hitler removed units from the Ardennes Front to reinforce the defence of Budapest and the line of the Danube north and south of the city.

Above: A map showing the short-lived 'Spring Awakening' offensive and the planned move towards Budapest, and the subsequent Soviet thrust towards Vienna, leading to the latter's capture in April 1945.

STAVKA ordered Marshal Theodor Ivanovich Tolbukin to prepare the forces of the 3rd Ukrainian Front for the coming battle of Budapest. Stalin's order had been stark: 'Take Budapest as quickly as possible.' The response was quick; the Red Army advanced into Hungary and on Christmas Eve 1944 its tanks burst into the suburbs of Buda, striking towards the landmark of the Hotel Gellert. The late-night shoppers at first took it for granted that the tanks were German, but once the Red Stars were spotted, there was panic. The hitherto peaceful streets became battlegrounds as the German Tigers rumbled across the bridges of the

Danube to close with the advancing armour of the 3rd Ukrainian Front, one of whose notable triumphs had been the active support of Marshal Tito in the capture of Belgrade the previous October. The Russian forces, consisting of three assault groups of tank, motorized and cavalry units, advanced but were then repulsed. Simultaneously, the 2nd Ukrainian Front of Marshal Rodion Yakovievich Malinovsky was crossing the Danube above Budapest. Two days after Christmas, the two formations met west of the city. Five German and four Hungarian divisions, with 800,000 civilians, were cut off and surrounded. Emissaries went forward to discuss the terms of capitulation.

To Hitler this was the ultimate heresy. There would be no capitulation. Budapest would be recaptured, not evacuated. This was never to be; the Russians' gigantic rocket assault blew apart the buildings and infrastructure of the ancient city, the onslaught orchestrated by the blare of Soviet loudspeakers urging the Hungarians to come out peacefully and join the Red Army. Those who had time pinned strips of red cloth to their uniforms. Others who did not were butchered.

DETRITUS OF DEFEAT

In vain, General Heinz Guderian, the acting Army Chief of Staff, urged the *Führer* to concentrate all his forces, including those withdrawn from the west after the debacle in the Ardennes, to defend the Oder. But Hitler, mesmerized above all by the threat to the oil resources around Lake Balaton, would have none of it.

The fact that the oil wells were no longer able to supply sufficient oil even to meet the requirements of Army Group South was brushed aside. What was needed, the *Führer* proclaimed, was 'the wider vision', adding: 'Hungary must be the objective. We will throw the

Below: Two *panzergrenadiers* from Sixth SS Panzer Army keep an eye out for the Soviet troops who they know will soon appear, driving forward towards Budapest. The fight for the capital was to be long and hard.

Russians back across the Danube and then there will be other victories.' It was Hitler's intention that General O. Wohler's Army Group South would trap and destroy the 3rd Ukrainian Front between Lake Balaton and the Danube. The major thrust would be launched by Sepp Dietrich's Sixth Panzer Army, now withdrawn from the Western Front. Dietrich would attack southeast from the northern end of Lake Balaton to a line on the Danube embracing Budapest-Baja. From south of the lake, advancing directly east, would come Second Panzer Army with a supporting attack to be launched northwards from the Yugoslavian border. Budapest would be taken and the Red Army front 'struck off the order of battle'.

In his memoirs Guderian, with uncharacteristic mildness, summed up the bitter clash between himself and Hitler: 'I was sceptical, since very little time had been allowed for preparation, and neither the troops nor the commanders possessed the same drive as in the old days.' But argument with Hitler proved fruitless. An order from *Führer* Headquarters (*Führerhauptquartier, FHQ*) had reached the *Wiking* Division's command post near Modlin on Christmas night, sent, Guderian later maintained, without his knowledge. The personnel of IV SS Panzer Corps were to be transported forthwith by rail to the Komarom area. Here they were to relieve IX SS Mountain Corps of *SS-Gruppenführer und Generalleutnant der Waffen-SS* (Lieutenant-General) Karl von Pfeffer-Wildenbruch, a veteran police general, who was now under threat from the encircling Soviet forces.

The men of *Germania* and *Westland* scarcely had time to breath before they were formed into two battle groups. The toughest assignment went to *Germania*, ordered forthwith to institute a frontal attack in the direction of Budapest. In darkness, *Westland* was to form up behind *Germania*, holding the position firm while *Germania* stormed ahead with enemy antitank guns, assault groups, and tanks forming its target.

Left: 'Royal' Tigers of the Sixth SS Panzer Army before the launch of the 'Spring Awakening' offensive in Hungary. The tanks were too little, too late; in any case they lacked fuel to manoeuvre properly in combat.

Left: The face of defeat – a *Waffen-SS panzergrenadier* in the closing months of the war. To the end, many stayed loyal to their oath to Hitler. Most were motivated by ideology, and they would fight 'Bolshevism' to the end.

Opinion was divided on the wisdom, not only of a frontal attack, but also of tying down a panzer group and battle group in one location. The decision to send *Westland* at first light into what turned out to be a heavily opposed uphill attack was at first successful, but all too soon the battalions were pinned down by heavy fire. It was then proposed to assail the Russians' weakest positions in the Pilis mountains, situated to the north of Budapest on the right bank of the Danube. The mountain network of caves, steep cliffs and hairpin bends proved useful as outposts and strongpoints for the Red Army. Along the winding roads eventually was to be seen the detritus of a German Army retreating in defeat, lorries and trucks abandoned, along with weapons and equipment. Marauding Soviet troops used the debris as cover.

DENTED MORALE

Even though units of the Red Army were now in sight of the suburbs of the Hungarian capital, IV SS Panzer

Corps received orders to shift position to the industrial and farming area of Szekesfehervar in the southwest. This is believed to have been on the personal orders of Hitler himself. It was from here that the next attempt to break the stranglehold on Budapest would be made. *SS-Obergruppenführer* (General) Gille, who from the beginning had been opposed to using Szekesfehervar as an operational base, had his fears confirmed when it became evident that the Russians had anticipated the move and heavily mined the area, resulting in a distinct lack of progress for the Germans. Nevertheless, Ullrich, as *Wiking*'s commander, urged forward the armoured group of *SS-Obersturmbannführer* (Lieutenant-Colonel) Hans Dorr of *Germania*, and by the evening they had broken through at a point where Russian manpower was thin on the ground.

A briefing at *Germania's* command post in Sarosd, earlier wrested from Russian hands, resulted in a serious loss to the Division. A direct hit by an antitank shell killed several officers, and severely wounded Hans Dorr, who later died of his injuries. This incident dented the morale of the division which, fortuitously, was restored by the capture of Szekesfehervar, at a time when the Russian Fifty-Seventh Guards Army had been chronically short of reinforcements and munitions. But nothing seemingly could now stop the final Russian assault on Budapest which was launched at around 07:00 hours on 29 January 1945 and, so it was rumoured, was likely to be hindered only by one battered cavalry division. The overall loss to *Wiking* and *Totenkopf* of men and materiel was bleeding the *Waffen-SS* dry. A slow countermove was set at naught by the strength of enemy fire, and the command post at Szekesfehervar had to be moved back. All resistance

Right: *Panzergrenadiers* shelter from Soviet artillery fire in their trench in Hungary. The Red Army had a massive superiority in artillery, and every attack was preceded by a lengthy bombardment.

Right: Towards the end of the war the *Waffen-SS* fought street by street, house by house, room by room, holding off retreat until the final moment. However, they could only delay the inevitable collapse of Germany.

collapsed. As a contributor to *History of the Second World War*, the American historian Earl K. Ziemke wrote:

'On the morning of February 11, Pfeffer-Wildenbruch issued orders for a breakout. In a gesture reminiscent of Paulus' promotion to Field-Marshal at Stalingrad, Hitler had conferred the Knight's Cross of the Iron Cross on him the day before. But the garrison was down to its last rations and ammunition, and split into two pockets, both too small for airdrops. On the night of the 11th the troops tried to force their way out along the Italian Boulevard while the staffs took a roughly parallel route through a subterranean drainage channel. Few even reached the suburbs. Of close to 30,000 Germans and Hungarians – 10,600 wounded were left behind – less than 700 reached the German lines.'

No Relief

In a rapid advance the Russians had encircled Szekesfehervar and from Hitler came the by now characteristically intransigent demand: 'Szekesfehervar is to be defended without regard for losses; the combat commander responsible is the commander of *Westland*.' Pleas for relief were impossible; contact could not be made with *Wiking* divisional HQ, which was situated some 18km (11 miles) west of Szekesfehervar. A reconnaissance regimental cycle platoon reported that encirclement of the town by the Russians was virtually complete. Then in recognition that obedience of the *Führer* order would amount to a death sentence for *Wiking, SS-Obergruppenführer* Gille at IV SS Panzer Corps authorized a withdrawal westwards together with the wounded. The Soviets' steamroller advance had found *Obersturmbannführer* (Lieutenant-Colonel) Franz Hack of *Westland* in the thick of it:

'In the course of the day, the Soviet Russians attack us frontally, supported by artillery and "Stalin organ" fire. The battle rages in and around the little town of Seregelyes … We captured a complete "Stalin organ" with tractor and ammunition. Our men from the

artillery and infantry gun units under *Hauptsturmführer* [Captain] Peter Wollseifer, turn the multiple mortar around and soon the Soviet Russians get a taste of area bombardment from their own rocket weapon.'

A key role in the withdrawal was played by 9th SS-Panzer-Division *Hohenstaufen*, which had also originally been recruited from foreign volunteers. It shifted its front to the northern part of Lake Balaton in order to hold the sector open for the *Wiking* Division. Within hours, the latter was able to find the protection of *Hohenstaufen*'s front. All points west were jammed, and powerful motorized forces encountered nothing more lethal than infantry small arms and several meagre supplies of ammunition.

The launch of Hitler's offensive, codenamed 'Spring Awakening', had begun on 18 February

when I and II SS Panzer Corps entrained from Wiesbaden, Koblenz and Bonn. Hitler had summoned smartly uniformed reserve forces which seemingly had a call on the most sophisticated weapons. But assembly was one thing; fast movement another. The progress of the new reserve formations had been much hindered by Allied air attacks and fuel shortages, so it was not until the beginning of March that Sepp Dietrich was able to assemble his forces between Lakes Balaton and Velencze. As well as two panzer corps, Sixth SS Panzer Army also had under its command two cavalry divisions and *Wiking* and *Totenkopf* of IV SS Panzer Corps, and a Hungarian infantry division. The plan was for the main attack to be made on 6 March with Sixth Army under General Hermann Balck, with Dietrich's 6th

SS Panzer Army on his right. Subsidiary attacks on the day before would be the responsibility of Army Group E across the Drava and Second Panzer Army to the south of Lake Balaton. As to the fate of Sixth SS Panzer Army, Sepp Dietrich later recounted:

'My left flanks [II SS Panzer Corps] had no success worth mentioning. The emplacements along the western bank of the Danube, the hard strong enemy, and the marshy terrain, impassable for tanks, prevented our advancing and attaining our goal ... The centre [I Panzer Corps and the cavalry divisions] reported good success; yet when tanks were employed to exploit the initial successes, the terrain proved completely impassable. The terrain, which was supposed to be frozen hard, and which General von Wohler had maintained to be passable, was wet and marshy ...'

Sixth SS Panzer Army was equipped with the MkVI Tiger II heavy battle tank – the 'Royal' or 'King' Tiger – massively armoured and mounting an 88mm (3.46in) gun. In addition, more than 600 tanks and self-propelled guns were in support of this bid to batter through the Soviet lines of Lake Velencze. All this weaponry, however sophisticated, proved useless, and the burnt-out hulks were left stranded in the water-logged plains. There was a general consensus that the 'Royal' Tigers had proved irrelevant; a sarcastic comment by the troops was that Hitler's *Schnorkel*-equipped U-boats would have been better. The coup de grace was delivered by Russia's artillery and attack aircraft.

The failure of the SS in Hungary caused consternation. Hitler, according to Guderian, who heard it from Wohler, was 'beside himself' and sent Himmler to find out what had gone wrong. The Führer, according to some accounts, remained obsessive about regaining the oilfields, until he was shown an aerial photograph depicting the sites as nothing but bomb craters. Surprisingly, perhaps, despite the fact that the entire Eastern Front was as good as lost, morale among SS troops apparently remained high, as did the sense of discipline and spirit of comradeship. *Wiking* Division's *SS-Obersturmführer* (Lieutenant) Eric Brorup recalled:

'My most memorable encounter took place on St Patrick's Day, 17 March 1945, near Szekesfehervar in Hungary. I was adjutant … to *SS-Sturmbannführer* [Major] Fritz Vogt, holder of the Knight's Cross with Oak Leaves. The Russians had started their offensive the day before, which was also Fritz Vogt's 27th birthday. Our unit was *SS-Panzer Aufklarungs Abteilung 5*.

I had established a command post in a small house and set up communications with a switchboard and radio while shells fell all around us. *SS-Obergruppenführer und General der Waffen-SS* [General] Herbert Otto Gille telephoned to congratulate Vogt on his birthday and to tell him he had just been awarded the Oak Leaves to his Knight's Cross. His face lit up and I said: "This calls for a drink!" We hoisted a few, then the supply officers showed up bearing some bottles of beer, and all the other officers found time to show up for a quick drink. All the while the war was going on around us.

One company commander was having some trouble with the enemy, so I suggested to Vogt that I go out and try to straighten things out. Vogt laughed and said: "What's the matter with you, do you feel like a hero today?" I answered that he had just got himself a new medal and should let others have a chance to win one. He replied: "Okay, but watch what you are doing!" By this time, of course, we had all had a good drink and were in excellent spirits!

I got an SdKfz 250/9 (a half track armoured personnel carrier with 20mm [0.79in] cannons mounted) and went into battle. We were firing high-explosive shells and it seemed easy, like shooting fish in a barrel.

Above: Sepp Dietrich (left), commander of 6th SS Panzer Army, of which the remnants of *Wiking* were a part. The last months of the war were spent by the division defending first Budapest, then Vienna.

Then the Russians brought up an antitank rifle and shot up my vehicle, forcing us to bail out. We ended up in hand-to-hand combat with them. I had a *Panzerfaust* antitank rocket but it wouldn't fire. I therefore used it like a club and cracked one Russian's head with it. I was in trouble, though. However, Fritz Vogt then appeared with a few more armoured personnel carriers and got me out. He told me to take a couple of hours off, and

later he and I went off alone on a reconnaissance behind enemy lines. I got the Iron Cross First Class for all this ...'

VIENNA THREATENED

By now the Russians held Budapest in a vice. Hitler sacked Wohler and replaced him with General Lothar Rendulic to head Army Group South. On 25 March the Russian breakthrough was all but complete and the next day the Russians went into the final phase which was the drive into Austria, the shortlived *Ostmark* province of the German *Reich*. Dietrich had pressed on to Vienna, his arrival greeted by a radio announcement stating that he had been appointed to defend the capital. Making the best of an impossible job in that city of shambles, he teamed up with Rendulic, who had hastened to join him from St Polten, east of Linz. High priority was given to the defence of Vienna by the *Waffen-SS*, although there was nothing that even remotely compared with the defensive systems that had existed in Buda and Pest. Rearguard detachments of Sixth SS Panzer Army, with elements of *Wiking*, *Leibstandarte* and the 17th Infantry Division, set up frequent ambushes, mined roads and blew bridges to hold off the Soviet Army. A hard time was given to the Soviet Sixth Guards Tank Army on the line of the river Leithe. The strength of army tank brigades was slashed to between 7 and 10 tanks, but it made little difference overall. The men of *Wiking* remained fanatic in adhering to their SS oath of allegiance and were determined to fight to the last gasp. Training sessions continued with the emphasis on hand-to-hand combat. Somehow supplies of food – 'of the highest quality', according to Peter Strassner – reached the Division. There were even instances of the German penchant for stockpiling being extended to replacement guns and tractors.

By now in the European theatre the fate of Hungary was no longer a major concern. Hitler had ordered that the main Russian assault force, crossing the Oder south of Stettin, should be opposed to the last man. His orders were carried out almost to the letter by 65 men from *Wallonien*; only 35 men survived. But the Russians were breasting the Oder and the threat of a Soviet assault on Berlin and the Elbe had become the new nightmare. On 16 April came the ultimate 'whistle in the dark'. This was the final order of the day to *Wiking*: 'If every soldier on the Eastern Front does his duty in these coming days and weeks, the last assault from Asia will be broken, exactly as the invasion by our enemy in the west will fail in the end in spite of everything. Berlin remains German, Vienna will be German again and Europe will never be Russian.'

SURRENDER PLANS

In isolated pockets, the Front had remained firm with the division holding off attacks in the Walkersdorf area, but a divisional order reached a pioneer battalion at noon on 7 May, ordering abandonment of its positions, since surrender was imminent. Indeed, that night Ullrich gave the order for withdrawal to the north behind an agreed demarcation line where the surrender was to be, not to Russian forces, but the Americans. During the long withdrawal south to Graz, *Westland* became separated for a while from the rest of the Division and was forced to fight it out when the Russians moved into the vacated territory. On the river Mur, the Russians were waiting with cavalry and T-34 tanks. Those who survived the onslaught made for the American lines at Radstad, north of the river. A note of irony was struck by the presence of a number of Russians who had been prisoners of the Germans and who were considerably concerned about their fate at the hands of the commissars. A plea that they should accompany the men of *Wiking* was turned down; there was no transport available to carry them. As Peter Strassner later reported:

'Just before the demarcation line ... *Oberführer* [Colonel] Ullrich released the commanders and officers from their oath and left them free to go into an uncertain imprisonment with the troops or to strike out into the mountains and attempt to reach their homes. He himself, he explained, preferred to remain with his men in order to fulfil their trust in

Right: The advance guard of a Soviet division moves cautiously through Budapest. The buildings on the street show the marks of battle – the Hungarian capital was the scene of hard fighting for some months.

the difficult times ahead. All of the assembled officers shared the view of their commander and went into American captivity ...'

In contrast to the treatment that they would undoubtedly have received from the Russians, the prisoners were treated with courtesy and the officers were allowed to keep their firearms. On 1 June, their transportation to a detention camp in Upper Bavaria began, and they remained there until September, when the detention camp was disbanded.

LAST RITES

SS-Standartenoberjunker Jan Munk of *Westland* was one of those attempting to form the so-called *Nibelungen* Division made up of *Volksturm* personnel, the German equivalent of Britain's Home Guard, drawn from all males between the ages of 16 and 60 who were not in the armed forces, but were capable of bearing arms. Munk found himself in a rural area some 29km (18 miles) from the Austrian border and 96km (60 miles) from Munich. He later recalled:

'I was given a company of Labour Corps boys, all 16 or 17 years old and as keen as mustard ... On 1 May at Eggenfelden near Vilsbiberg, I went with my boys to the edge of a forest. We had to hold that position. We saw about a dozen American tanks approaching, moving in single file along a narrow road. I managed to disable the first one, but I could see that our position was hopeless. I sent all the boys away to make their own way home ...'

Not every unit of *Wiking* was a spent force; there were remnants whose retreat from the battle fronts brought them to the final showdown in Berlin. That the foreign legions fought fiercely to the last did not necessarily mean fanatical devotion to the Nazi cause. To the German soldier, surrender would most likely mean a prison camp, but to the foreign collaborators there loomed trial at the vengeful hands of their own people, bitter from years of occupation, followed by

Left: A Soviet patrol hunts for any stragglers or hidden snipers in the ruins of Budapest. They use dogs to help detect any hidden humans – civilians were also trapped beneath the rubble.

the very real possibility of the firing squad. All was now set for the capture of Berlin itself.

On 16 January 1945, and unbeknown to most Berliners, Hitler had returned, at first to take up residence in the Reich Chancellery building, which was once intended as the symbol of a proud rebuilt capital city. The gaunt edifice, now surrounded by a moonscape of craters and rubble, was itself pounded and pockmarked by bomb blasts. On 30 January, Hitler delivered his last speech over the radio, and thereafter took refuge increasingly in the concrete shelter built in the Chancellery garden. Eventually he moved permanently in what was the 13th and last *Führer* Headquarters. Buried 17m (55ft) below ground, the bunker was built in two storeys with exterior walls 1.8m (6ft) thick and a 2.4m (8ft) thick concrete canopy topped with 9m (30ft) of earth. The *Führerbunker* was divided into 18 cramped rooms, from which the means of contact with the outside world had dwindled to a modest switchboard and one radio transmitter, as well as one radio-telephone link with the Army High Command headquarters at Zossen.

In the north of Berlin there now came Rokossovsky with the 2nd Belorussian Front, in the centre Zhukov with the 1st Belorussian Front and, in the south, Koniev's 1st Ukrainian Front. The race for the German capital was on, heralded by three red flares soaring into the sky above the Kustrin bridgehead. The German frontline was engulfed with the furious bombardment of 20,000 artillery pieces that set forests ablaze. This was the harbinger of Zhukov's offensive. As Koniev advanced in the south, Zhukov's Red Army hordes struck out across the Oder on rafts and in boats. The Oder line was ripped open on a 70km (44-mile) front. By 20 April, Red Army troops had breached the outer northwest defensive perimeter of Berlin. The city itself was dotted with slit trenches and isolated pillboxes which had been erected far too late to have much effect. Although the cuttings, culverts

Left: The countless bodies of *Waffen-SS* men left behind in the snows of Russia, not counting the thousands taken prisoner, meant that the best of Germany's menfolk had been lost to her by the time she needed them most.

and overhead railways of Berlin's transportation system formed ready-made obstacles and barriers, there was no one there to man them.

WITHOUT MERCY

In the war's closing days, apart from two under-strength army divisions, the defence of Berlin was in the hands of 11th SS-Panzergrenadier-Freiwilligen-Division *Nordland*, along with scattered French and Latvian *Waffen-SS*, and the tattered remnants of *Wiking*. These were the once proud and sometimes arrogant products of Steiner's barrack squares. The ignominious task of these once-haughty formations was to muster as many *Volksturm* as they could dragoon into the last-ditch defence. Lists of those *Volksturm* liable for service had previously been compiled by local Nazi Party organizations and their politically reliable officers appointed by *Gauleiters* (provincial governors) and their subordinate *Kreisleiters*.

Eventually the *Volksturm* battalions together amounted to 15 million men, but few were equipped either with materiel or the experience to confront a determined enemy. Nevertheless, whether baby faces or gnarled veterans, they were thrust into the front line. That any effective defence of Berlin remained was mere illusion. A bizarre scheme concocted by the *Hitler Jugend* leader, Artur Axman, to smuggle Hitler out between a gap in the Russian lines under the protection of *Nordland* was angrily rejected by the *Führer*. By then, at last recognizing defeat, Hitler ended his life on 30 April. His last testament served as a final vicious kick. He had been betrayed; the German people had proved unequal to and unworthy of his leadership. They would deserve the dire future that he foresaw for them. Berlin was now destined to become the graveyard of what remained of the *Waffen-SS*.

The end for these men was possibly more bearable than the particularly horrific fate reserved for those from Estonia, the Baltic republic which had previously been under Soviet control, and whose Grenadier Division had fought with *Wiking*. In the autumn of 1944, despite a ferocious defence against the Red Army along the Estonian–Russian border, the Estonians were overrun, driven out and forced into

retreat alongside their German allies. The pursuit had
first been into Silesia and finally Czechoslovakia, where
the men were cornered and then butchered without
mercy. Those who did manage to escape westwards surrendered willingly to Anglo–American forces. Not all
those who served in the non-Germanic contingents of
Wiking came home to the sort of welcome they had
hoped for. Ornulf Bjornstad, who had come back from
the Eastern Front after serving in the Caucasus and the
Ukraine along with his comrades in *Germania*, would
recall after the war had ended:

'At the start of the war we made it clear to everyone
that we were fighting with the Germans because they
offered the best hope of beating communism. I had a
lot of encouragement from my family and friends. But
when the war started going against Germany their attitude changed to hostility against the whole German
cause. This change of attitude dated from the defeat at
Stalingrad in 1943 and the subsequent retreat.'

POST-WAR RECKONING

A mere handful of veterans at that time constituted his
only friends. He was among those who did not merely
encounter the cold shoulder of disapproval. In a new
post-war mood, Norway became intent on revenge
against those tainted with Nazi collaboration. Ornulf
Bjornstad was arrested, brought to trail and sentenced
to five years of hard manual labour.

Apart from disillusion and the perils of an uncertain
future in a shattered land, it could be argued that the
lucky ones were those men and youths turned loose
amid the smoking ruins of the *Reich* capital. Not for
them was the dreadful fate of being far from home in
a frozen hell, crushed to bloody pulp under the tracks
of tanks or incinerated by blazing fuel from burning
panzers. There had also been those who vanished to
rot in the hell of Soviet jails. For as long as 30 years
after the war's end, it was believed that there were still
prisoners in Russia who would never be released. Any

**Right: One of the last photographs of the *Waffen-SS* in
action in World War II, showing men of the 6th SS
Panzer Army accompanied by a Panther tank during yet
another local counterattack against the Red Army.**

sympathy for them must, of course, be tempered by knowledge of the atrocities committed by the *Waffen-SS* (including the various units of *Wiking*) on the Eastern Front. As for pointing the finger of blame at those responsible for the hideous waste of young lives, one man – who was in a unique position to know – had few doubts. Field Marshal Erich von Manstein, agreed by many historians to have been Germany's most outstanding military commander during World War II, made the judgement in his memoirs:

'… bravely as the *Waffen SS* divisions always fought, and fine though their achievements may have been, there is not the least doubt that it was an inexcusable mistake to set them up as a separate military organization. Hand-picked replacements which could have filled the posts of NCOs in the army were expended on a quite inadmissible scale in the *Waffen-SS*, which in general paid a toll of blood incommensurate with its actual gains. Naturally this cannot be laid at the door of the SS troops themselves. The blame for such unnecessary consumption of manpower must lie with the men who set up these special units for purely political motives, in the face of opposition from all the competent army authorities.

In no circumstances must it be forgotten, however, that the *Waffen-SS*, like the good comrades they were, fought shoulder to shoulder with the army at the front and always showed themselves courageous and reliable. Without doubt a large proportion of them would have been only too glad to be withdrawn from the jurisdiction of a man like Himmler and incorporated into the army.'

For those who had dreamt of a brighter future for their country, and who had fought with the *Waffen-SS* for genuinely idealistic and selfless reasons, the fairest judgement will surely be these men had been woefully misguided and misled. In their unswerving dedication, they had at least shown themselves to be worthy of an infinitely better cause.

Right: A knocked-out halftrack on the streets of Berlin in May 1945, her dead crew lying alongside. Often wrongly attributed to *Wiking*, it in fact carries the markings of the *Nordland* Division, which also recruited foreign volunteers.

CHAPTER EIGHT

KEY FIGURES

Although Felix Steiner was the first commander of the *Wiking* Division, Herbert Gille made it his own. The division has always had a certain notoriety due to its composition of largely non-German volunteers, but this is compounded by Josef Mengele's war service.

FELIX STEINER

Any account of the career of Felix Steiner has to consist of more than his service as commander of the 5th SS-Panzer-Division *Wiking* and subsequently of III SS (German) Panzer Corps. For it was Steiner's radical approach to methods of training that helped the *Waffen-SS* become what the historian Gerald Reitlinger described as 'the most efficient of all the military training systems of the Second World War'. Born on 23 May 1896 in Stalluponen, East Prussia, of an Austrian emigrant family, Steiner went to war in 1914 with the 5th East Prussian Infantry Regiment No 41 *Van Boyení* and fought at Tannenburg where he was severely wounded. After serving as company leader in a machine-gun battalion, he was engaged in the thick of the fighting in the massive German offensives of Spring 1918, both in Flanders and also in France.

Three years after the armistice, Steiner was back in service, now with the *Reichswehr*, the post-World War I German Army, where he became adjutant to an infantry regiment with the rank of captain. Promotion followed to the rank of major as a staff member of the

Left: Felix Steiner (left) shown when he was commander of III SS Panzer Corps, awarding the Iron Cross to an Estonian volunteer, *Obersturmbannführer* (First Lieutenant) Harald Riipalu.

Reichswehr's training command. His interest in radical methods of training sprung from searing experiences in the Kaiser's war, in which he believed that there had been needless and wanton sacrifice of lives. The opportunity to bring about concrete changes came with the rise of Hitler and the creation of the *SS-Verfügungstruppen*, which, in its early stages, served as the *Führer*'s praetorian guard before going on to achieve an increased military complexity.

Steiner's early role in the *Verfügungstruppen* was in the development of the 3rd Battalion of the SS-Regiment *Deutschland* which was stationed in Munich and had its training camp at Dachau. Here he applied his military training to the men with the ethos of his own personal motto 'Sweat saves blood'. Furthermore, he claimed that with *Deutschland*, 'a new soldier spirit grew from the beginning'. At first the number of professional soldiers who joined the SS were few and they were disdained by those whose attitude was firmly entrenched in the strictly conservative Prussian tradition. Steiner's conviction was that the future belonged to small, élite units that would fight independently, harnessing all that modern technology could provide. His decision to do away with barrack-square drill in favour of shorter periods of combat training with live ammunition was at first greeted with derision. But those who opposed Steiner were obliged to change

Above: Felix Steiner in thoughtful mood. Before commanding *Wiking* Divsion, Steiner had led the *Deutschland* regiment in the SS-VT Division during the Polish and French campaigns.

their views with the conversion of Hitler himself to Steiner's creed. Indeed, Hitler had been totally unaware of how quickly Steiner's revolutionary style of training had advanced when in 1939 the new tactics were demonstrated by *Deutschland* at the Munsterlager training area. The *Führer* had been searching the ground with his binoculars, enquiring when the attack would start. Steiner replied that it had been in progress for 20 minutes. It was at this point that the assault troops appeared, moving forwards rapidly, neither pausing nor allowing themselves to be pinned down by fire. The men, who had covered 3km (1.9 miles) in

under 20 minutes, appeared fresh and tireless, ready for close-quarter battle with hand grenades and demolition charges. Furthermore, to assist the speed of their advance, they carried machine pistols rather than rifles. Every bit as delighted as Hitler with the effectiveness of Steiner's methods of training was Heinrich Himmler, who was keen to secure all credit for himself as *Reichsführer-SS*. But not everyone was happy about Steiner's increasing involvement with the *Waffen-SS*. A note of jealousy can be discerned in the remark of Paul Hausser, the retired *Reichswehr* officer who had been instructed by Hitler in 1935 to form an officer cadet school after joining the SS the year before. He acidly described Steiner as 'Himmler's favourite baby'.

During the Polish campaign at the outbreak of World War II, the 2800-strong regiment *Deutschland* was, along with other units of the *SS-Verfügungstruppen*, attached to Panzer-Division *Kempf.* On its transfer to the west, the regiment engaged with a French division in Holland. It broke through in the area of Walcheren island on the north bank of the Scheldt estuary, taking Vlissingen at the mouth of the river. Just how successful Steiner had become in building up a totally loyal and fearless cadre of troops was demonstrated strikingly during the early stages of the evacuation of the British Expeditionary Force (BEF) from Dunkirk in May 1940. George Stein in his book *Waffen-SS* writes of 'one of the earliest recorded examples of the fanatically tenacious almost suicidal behaviour that characterized the combat performance of the *Waffen-SS* throughout the war'. A British brigade had thrown the SS out of the town of St Venant, which had been serving as a vital passage for BEF units preparing for a rapid withdrawal across the river Lys. Pursuit was hampered when forward elements of 3rd Panzer Division became bogged down. Well in advance of any German unit, SS-Regiment *Deutschland* thrust through successfully to the river. Steiner, as regimental commander, ordered his 3rd Battalion to attack across the water

Right: Herbert Otto Gille, second commander of the *Wiking* Division, had an undistinguished start to his career in the *Waffen-SS*. He had previously served as an officer in World War I, winning the Iron Cross.

with two batteries of artillery in support. The men of *Deutschland*, undaunted by vastly superior odds, fired on the English tanks at distances of under 4.5m (15ft) with rifles, machine guns and antitank rifles or pitched hand grenades at a few yards range into the face of the oncoming tanks. Retaliation by other British tanks emerging from the north was greeted with ferocious opposition. Further blood-letting slowed the British withdrawal. This and other actions in France and Belgium brought Steiner the Knight's Cross as well as promotion to the rank of *SS-Brigadeführer und Generalmajor* (Major-General).

With this promotion came a crucial assignment at the prompting of Heinrich Himmler: formation of a new motorized SS division which would draw on the volunteers of most western and north European countries. The eventual result was the *SS-Wiking*, destined for divisional status. In support of *Wiking*, Steiner claimed that its creation paved the way for the 'historically and politically correct idea of a Europe with a common destiny which embraced all European volunteers and bound them together in spirit'. The lessons learnt by the men of *Wiking* on Steiner's training grounds were further translated into highly effective action towards the end of June 1941 when 'Operation Barbarossa', the invasion of the Soviet Union, was already underway. Subordinate to III Panzer Corps, *Wiking* participated in the success of a speedy advance towards Cholm, a small town lying at the confluence of the Lovat and Kunya rivers in marshy territory south of Lake Ilmen. Garrisoned by 3500 men from a variety of different units, the town had been quickly surrounded.

Lightning attacks during the second battle for Rostov and the thrust to the Kuban in August 1942, followed by solid achievements in the Caucasus, led to the award of the Oak Leaves to Steiner's Knights Cross. In May 1943, Steiner was charged by Hitler with the formation of III (German) SS Panzer Corps in a year when the situation on the Eastern Front was becoming critical. At first the corps had some success in blocking a heavy Russian incursion into the bridgehead at Oranienbaum (now Lomonosov), situated on the southern edge of the Gulf of Finland immediately to the west of Leningrad. But following the intervention

of the Soviet Second Shock Army at the bridgehead, the corps suffered devastatingly from a heavy 65-minute artillery bombardment. It was then forced to withdraw west to Narva on the border with Estonia, where fierce fighting continued throughout the summer. The Oak Leaves with Swords which Steiner received was just about the only consolation for him until the war's end. Indeed, he could count himself extremely fortunate to have collected the honour at all and not to have suffered a gruesome fate. On the morning of 20 July 1944, Hitler had held a military briefing at the Wolf's Lair (*Wolfsschanze*), a massive concrete blockhouse serving as FHQ at Rastenburg in East Prussia. A bomb, planted under the conference table by a group of conspirators who intended to kill Hitler and seek peace terms with the Allies, had exploded. The *Führer*, however, survived. Revenge was swift and terrible. The subsequent wave of arrests and barbaric executions by slow strangulation swept up 2 field marshals and 16 generals. Other arrests and killings also followed. Steiner, along with many in the SS, had called for the removal of Hitler on the grounds that the *Führer* was mentally deranged, but he was not actively involved in the plot. By some miracle, Steiner survived the subsequent witch-hunt.

October saw Steiner forced by a bout of jaundice to delegate command to *SS-Obergruppenführer* (General) George Keppler. After recovery came command in the New Year of Eleventh Army. This was an impressive title for a tattered outfit which was to consist largely of the remnants of an SS police division summoned for an ineffectual attack south of Stettin. Hitler pinned his faith on Steiner for the last-ditch defence of Berlin in the closing weeks of the war. The *Führer* elevated Steiner's command to an *Armee Abteilung* (army detachment), giving him three scratch divisions and the ghosts of a panzer corps. With these, Steiner was to attack south from Eberswalde on the Finow Canal, 24km (15 miles) north of Berlin. To his directive Hitler

Right: A portrait of Gille when divisional commander of *Wiking*. He had worked his way up from command of the division's artillery regiment, winning the Knight's Cross in October 1942. Note the prominent *Wiking* cuff band.

added: 'Officers who do not accept this order without reservation are to be arrested and shot instantly. You yourself I make responsible with your head for its execution.' Those who refused to furnish troops to Steiner would be 'dead within five hours'. The order was impossible to carry out. One of the divisions, the 4th SS *Polizei* Division, not only had just two battalions, but was also unarmed. Others were already tied down and their removal would leave the Front unprotected. Even though hastily supplied with a few thousand men of the *Luftwaffe* ground staff by way of reinforcements, Steiner stayed put. He later declared: 'I did not want to lose a single man in an enterprise doomed to crushing disaster from the start. The plan of attack had been established on bases which existed only in the imagination of the Reich Chancellery bunker.'

After an outburst of incoherent rage, Hitler returned to relative lucidity and issued another order to Steiner to establish a bridgehead across the Ruppihner Canal, on the route to the capital. Steiner, reasoning that it did not matter whether the bridgehead was established or not, obeyed the order. As it turned out, it was not large enough for tanks, and the Russians attacking from three sides ground to a halt. By this time Steiner was nursing a fond hope that the defeated Germans might team up with the Western Allies and thus turn against the Russians. But his own role in the defence of Berlin ceased abruptly. Hitler dismissed him. Within days, Steiner had quietly marched his men to the British lines.

His devotion to the men of his former division remained a byword. One example was later provided by the memories of a Swedish volunteer who had served with both the *Wiking* and *Nordland* Divisions throughout the Russian campaigns and during the battle for Berlin. The two men had encountered one another on the Oder Front in March 1945.

'As he approached me, his stern features brightened into a beaming smile. He had recognized me. And yet it was almost a year since I had taken part in a deputation from all ranks of the division which had greeted him at Narva on his birthday. Since then he had seen innumerable new faces and yet he recognized mine. He called me by my name.'

Until his death in Munich on 12 May 1966, Felix Steiner kept fully in touch with his old comrades and was a frequent figure at SS reunions. Released from prison on 27 April 1948, he wrote *The Volunteer*, an account of his war. He stoutly maintained until the end that 'the war against Bolshevism' had been justified.

HERBERT OTTO GILLE

Herbert Otto Gille, both as second commander of the *Wiking* Division and subsequently of IV SS Panzer Corps, had an early apprenticeship in the army which he joined as a teenager. Born on 8 March 1897 at Bad Gandersheim, he attended the military college in Bensbergen near Cologne. In the spring of 1914 he was transferred to the military college at Gros Lichterfelde in Berlin, later the training ground of many future members of the *Waffen-SS*.

Within a year Gille had reached the rank of lieutenant and he served in field artillery, where he was commended for his command of a platoon and battery, receiving both the Iron Cross First and Second Class and the Combatants Cross of Honour. At the close of the war he could see no advantage in staying in the army, and in March 1919 resigned as a First Lieutenant. For 15 years he worked in agriculture, but in May 1934 joined the *SS-Verfügungstruppen*, where he soon attained the rank of *SS-Obersturmführer* (First Lieutenant) and was appointed to command a platoon, followed by a machine-gun company. During the second year of the war he was transferred to Heuberg, where Felix Steiner was in the process of shaping the future *Wiking* Division and was looking for officer material who could serve in it.

Although he took part in the campaign in the West in 1940 and subsequently was awarded the German Cross in Gold, it was not until the summer of 1942 that Gille made a significant mark. That came with his leadership of a unit, in a forward position, in the Kuban area well to the southeast of Rostov, and involving forces of *Nordland* and *Germania*. A notable achievement was the securing of the Kuban after heavy fighting at a key railway junction at Krapotkin, where a 4000-strong Russian column was routed. This would earn him the Knight's Cross on 8 October 1942 and

also, as *SS-Oberführer* (Colonel), the overall command of 5th SS-Artillery-Regiment *Wiking*.

In August 1942 Gille – with *Wiking*, at the head of LVII Panzer Corps, with forces that included the 5th SS Artillery Regiment – was in action against furious enemy opposition from the area of Tuapse, located directly on the eastern edge of the Black Sea, penetrating the northwest and southwest of the Maykop oil region. On 9 November of that year, Gille was further promoted to *SS-Brigadeführer und General-Major der Waffen-SS* (Major-General).

During the following May Felix Steiner quit *Wiking* to take over III (Germanic) SS Panzer Corps. Gille was promoted to command the recently designated SS-Panzergrenadier-Division *Wiking*. It was an appointment not without controversy; there was some feeling that the new incumbent lacked sufficient experience for the post. As for his men, they came to regard him as a strict disciplinarian, who at the same time deliberately cultivated an air of informality which earned him the title 'Papa' Gille. A reassuring figure, he invariably

Above: Gille (left) watches the progress of the battle for Kowel with his *Wiking* Division staff. He was later promoted to command IV SS Panzer Corps, of which his old division was part.

sported a favourite gnarled walking stick. During his time, Gille particularly impressed *Untersturmführer* Peter Neumann of *Wiking*:

'... It is the first chance I've had of seeing him at such close quarters. He breakfasted in our Mess. He struck me as being extraordinarily simple and friendly. They say that on duty he's a hard man. But he did not strike me as at all severe ... Quite tall, carrying his 50-odd years lightly, slightly balding, he has the red face and nose of a *bon vivant*. His tortoiseshell glasses increase the impression of infectious good nature he seems to exude.'

In addition, Gille possessed a talent for organization as well as an iron nerve, qualities which were particularly in evidence during the perilous evacuation in January–February 1944 of the Korsun pocket, and the crossing of the icy waters of the Gniloi Tikitsch. Immediately following this breakout, he flew to the *Führer* HQ and received his Oakleaves with Swords.

By this time, German manpower was seriously haemorrhaging and the plight of the city of Kovel in the Ukraine had to take urgent precedence over supplies of reinforcements. Following the entrance of *Wiking* to Kovel on 16 March 1944, the city was encircled by the Russians, and it was Gille's assignment to fortify it. But the Front could only be stabilized; the consolation for Gille was that he was bestowed another decoration – the Oakleaves, Swords and Diamonds – of which he was the 12th recipient.

The division was exhausted, and parts of it were withdrawn to a training area in Poland. On regaining its strength Gille, having taken command of IV SS Panzer Corps, took part in the heavy defensive fights around Warsaw. On Christmas Eve 1944 the corps, under Gille, with the rank of *SS-Obergruppenführer und General der Waffen-SS* (General), was directed by Hitler to quit the severely threatened Warsaw Front and move 805km (500 miles) south to Budapest's Lake Balaton.

On New Year's Day, the *Wiking* and *Totenkopf* Divisions, supported by infantry, sped to Budapest airport in a bid to rescue 45,000 German soldiers and SS men. But an order from Fourth Army bent on surrounding 10 Russian divisions north of Balaton led to the withdrawal of Gille's corps. It was a move which would prove disastrous; the Russians had the breathing space to stiffen their resources, and by the end of the month the attack was scrapped. The Red Army moved in on Pest and the final collapse of the Germans was inevitable. On 8 May 1945, Gille passed into captivity and was released three years later.

He spent his remaining years running a small bookshop, as well as founding the veterans' magazine, called *Wiking Ruf* (*Wiking Call*). He died at Stemmen, near Hanover, of a heart attack on 26 December 1966, his funeral attended by more than 800 of his former comrades in *Wiking*.

JOHANNES-RUDOLF MUHLENKAMP

Johannes-Rudolf Muhlenkamp became commander of *Wiking* in succession to Herbert Gille in August 1944.

Indisputably one of the most able and daring tank men, as well as being a born leader and great inspiration to his men, Muhlenkamp was brought up in Braunschweig, where he was educated at the *Junkerschule*. He joined the SS with the number 86,065 and volunteered at the age of 24 for service in SS-Regiment *Germania*. He went to war with the regiment in Poland in 1939 with the rank of *SS-Untersturmführer* (Lieutenant). As he was already highly regarded by his superiors, Muhlenkamp was earmarked for fast promotion and, with the rank of SS-*Haupsturmführer* (Captain), was appointed to take over the command of the *SS-Aufklarungs Abteilung* (or reconnaissance unit) of the *Germania* Regiment.

came. The first one of its kind, it was designated *SS-Panzer Abteilung 5*, of SS-Division *Wiking*. The objective for the *Panzer Abteilung* in July 1942 was Rostov, which was to be assaulted with around 69 medium and heavy tanks, backed by infantry and supply services. The leader, known to his men as '*Hannes*', was in the fore-front of the surprise thrust where, under cover of the western flank, the *Panzer Abteilung* with two mounted assault companies pushed through at first light. The antitank ditches provided cover for the following infantry. Then it was on to Rostov itself. By 23 July, *Oberkommando der Wehrmacht* (OKW) was able to report: 'Units of the army, the *Waffen-SS* and Slovakian troops, supported by the *Luftwaffe*, have broken through Rostov's strongly defended, deeply emplaced defence positions along the whole front and after hard fighting have taken the important transport and port city.' In recognition of his contribution to the capture of Rostov, Muhlenkamp was awarded the Knight's Cross, and *SS-Panzer Abteilung 5* became a panzer regiment.

In April 1944, the breakthrough to Kovel, 256km (160 miles) southeast of Warsaw, had Muhlenkamp under fire all the way, breaking through to the north-west of the city against the stiffest resistance. SS-*Panzer Abteilung 5* this time recorded the destruction of 208 of the enemy's tank arm. Fiery retaliation to the Russians' massive assault on the Kovel-Lubin rail line served to stem the enemy breakthrough to Warsaw. Between 4 August and 5 September 1944, Russian losses of equip-ment, captured or destroyed by the regiment, would amount to 151 tanks, 19 assault guns, 13 self-propelled gun carriers, 176 guns, 94 machine guns, and 5 air-craft. These were achievements for which 'Hannes' Muhlenkampf was decorated, as the 596th recipient, with the Oak Leaves to his Knight's Cross. In August he also took over the command of *Wiking* from Herbert Gille with the rank of *SS-Standartenführer* (Colonel).

His subsequent appointment of Inspector of Panzer Troop, on the personal recommendation of Guderian, meant the *Wiking* post had to be relinquished. The task of commander passed to Karl Ullrich. Muhlenkamp's military career ended at the Oder Front. He was severely wounded on 5 February 1945 while in com-mand of 32nd SS Panzergrenadier Division, and he

Above: Gille (left) with Leon Degrelle (second from right) and Lieutenant-General Lieb (second left) with the German press chief Dr Dietrich after the successful breakout from the Korsun pocket.

He saw action first in France and then in the Balkans before being transferred to Russia. During the push towards Moscow in the summer of 1941, Muhlenkamp – with Paul Hausser – was seriously wounded when he took the full force of a Russian grenade launcher. A period in a Berlin hospital, dur-ing which he was awarded the Iron Cross in Gold, also saw promotion to *SS-Sturmbannführer* (Major). Then the order to establish the *Waffen-SS Panzer-Abteilung*

was taken prisoner by the Allies. He died in October 1986, after many years of ill health.

KARL ULLRICH

Unlike most of his senior colleagues, *SS-Standartenführer* (Colonel) Karl Ullrich, who was the last commander of SS-*Wiking*, did not spend his war totally with the Division. At the same time as graduating in civil engineering after study in Wurzburg, he was active as an enthusiastic member of the SA (*Sturm Abteilung* – Storm Troopers) and latterly the *Allegemeine-SS* (General SS). His military training was undertaken in the *Reichswehr*, but Ullrich eagerly grasped the opportunity to join the *SS-Verfügungstruppen*. He took infantry instruction in Munich and then underwent officers' training at the *Junkerschule Braunschweig*. Anxious to take full advantage of his early studies, Ullrich undertook further courses in engineering, learning its relevance to military usage. He joined an *SS-Pioneersturmbann* (Pioneer Detachment), eventually assuming company command and undergoing his baptism of fire in Poland at the start of World War II. In the ranks of the *SS-Verfügungstruppen* he saw action in the Netherlands, northern France and Yugoslavia, afterwards gaining both classes of the Iron Cross.

Ullrich's next significant appointment was as company commander of the Pioneer Battalion of the SS 'Death's Head' Division, *Totenkopf,* which in June 1941 was attached, for the invasion of Russia, to 4th Panzer Group in the vanguard of Field Marshal Wilhelm

Below: Karl Ullrich (right), the final commander of *Wiking***, with Otto Baum while both were serving with the** *Totenkopf* **Division at the battle of Kursk in July 1943. He was captured by the Americans at the end of the war.**

Ritter von Leeb's Army Group North. With promotion to *SS-Sturmbannführer* (Major), Ullrich took over the command of 3rd SS-Panzergrenadier-Regiment 6 *Theodor Eicke*. One of Ullrich's most distinguished acts of service to the 'Death's Head' Division occurred early in 1942, when the forces of *Totenkopf* were among those encircled at Demyansk, along one of the most sensitive sectors of Army Group North, halfway between Moscow and Leningrad. A vital defensive role to stem a major Russian breakthrough was assigned to *Totenkopf*, the nucleus of the mixed force of the army and *Waffen-SS* formations which were surrounded in the Demyansk pocket. The *Totenkopf* commander, Theodor Eicke, recommended to Hitler that Ullrich should receive the Knight's Cross for his heroism at the head of his pioneer battalion. He received confirmation of his award by radio from Hitler's headquarters. The Russian attack faltered, thanks to a *Luftwaffe* airlift in which, over a 10-week period, up to 150 flights a day ferried in 66,000 tonnes (65,000 tons) of supplies and lifted out 34,500 wounded. The men in the Demyansk pocket were relieved in the last week of April 1942.

During the night 7/8 July 1943, in preparation for the massive tank battle at Kursk, the assault groups of *Leibstandarte-SS Adolf Hitler*, *Das Reich* and *Totenkopf* stormed a network of antitank positions, machine-gun nests, bunkers and trenches. It was an assault which sent the Russians reeling, an initiative seized upon by 3rd Battalion of 1st Panzergrenadier Regiment, now commanded by *SS-Standartenführer* (Colonel) Karl Ullrich. The regiment cleared the sector's last Russian bunkers and sped towards the Psel River, which barred the advance. With a bridgehead firmly established on the river's north bank by Ullrich's panzergrenadiers, the way was laid open for an attack on the Russian rear.

In October of the following year and with German fortunes in terminal decline, Ullrich ('Ulli' to his men) took over the command of *Wiking* 'a good universally popular commander', according to Peter Strassner. The rapid switch of *Wiking* to Hungary found Ullrich fighting alongside his former comrades in *Totenkopf* as part of Sepp Dietrich's 6th SS Panzer Army. 'Operation Spring Awakening' (*Frühlingserwachen*) opened on 6 March in heavy snow; it lasted precisely one week.

Above: Count Christian Frederik von Schalburg volunteered for the SS-Regiment *Nordland*, serving in *Wiking* before taking command of the *Freikorps Danmark*. He was killed in action in June 1942.

Totenkopf was shattered beyond repair and *Wiking* was surrounded. Ullrich, preferring to disobey Hitler's orders to stand firm but willing to obey Dietrich, struck out westward. Taken prisoner of war by the Americans, Karl Ullrich served a three-year sentence and was released on 18 September 1948. During his retirement Ullrich made a contribution to a three-volume illustrated history of the *Totenkopf* Division.

LEON DEGRELLE

Leon Degrelle, the best known of the non-Germans to serve with *Wiking*, spent much of World War II on the Russian Front with his legion of Walloon volunteers. A

handsome and charismatic figure but totally without military experience, he displayed considerable resource and courage on the Eastern Front, after this rising from the rank of *Schütze* (Private) to *Obersturmbannführer* (Lieutenant-Colonel).

The son of a prosperous brewer from the small town of Bouillon in the Belgian Ardennes, he attended the University of Louvain where, as well as gaining his Doctorate in Law, he was active in politics, attracted especially to the radical wing of the Catholic Party. The Party was represented in many of the short-lived Belgian governments of the 1920s and 1930s. Having become a professional journalist, he took over the running of a small Catholic publishing house called Christus Rex, producing mass-circulation periodicals, literature and pamphlets. He went on to pedal a populist message of authoritarian political reform, backed by those who seethed with impatience at what they saw as the failure of the governing parties to produce an effective response to Belgium's social and economic problems. An effective orator and rabble-rouser, Degrelle attracted adherents primarily from the middle class: former soldiers from World War I, tradesmen and shopkeepers who were then suffering from the prevailing economic depression, together with an assortment of discontented right-wingers.

The movement's high spot was the General Election of May 1936. On a frankly populist ticket, Degrelle adopted the slogan 'A clean Belgium for clean Belgians'; the party's symbol was a broom. During the campaign, his followers paraded with canes, razors and loaded clubs, facing sabre-wielding mounted police. The Rexists won 21 seats from a total of 202. He next organized a march on Brussels, modelled on Mussolini's 1992 March on Rome which had swept Il Duce to power. Few turned out on the streets to witness what turned into a farce and a major tactical blunder. In a Brussels by-election in April 1937 Degrelle stood unsuccessfully against the Catholic Prime Minister,

Left: Leon Degrelle, head of the Belgian Rexist Party, had a colourful career with his *Legion Wallonien*, including surviving the Korsun pocket. He escaped to Spain at the end of the war, where he lived until his death in 1994.

Paul van Zeeland. Faced with disintegrating support, Degrelle set his face against Catholicism and remodelled the Rexist movement into a blatantly pro-Fascist affair. Alienated voters, mindful of events in Hitler's Germany, saw the Rexists as a disruptive rabble of little substance and by September 1939 they were regarded as little more than a truly spent force.

On the eve of the German invasion of 10 May 1940, Degrelle was arrested by the Belgian authorities and interned in France, along with other supporters, as a suspected member of a fifth column of pro-German sympathizers. He later alleged he was beaten and tortured in captivity, ending up in a concentration camp at Vernet in southern France. Amid the chaos of the German occupation, his release was secured by fellow Rexists. He next announced his intention of forming a government, confidently asserting that Hitler, whom he had met briefly in 1936, would be willing to support him. Such a friend, he confidently asserted, would help to fulfil his dream of recreating the 15th and 16th century Burgundian Empire in which Belgium would embrace large areas of both the Netherlands and northern France. In the wake of the German invasion in 1940, the remnants of the demoralized Rexists, seeing the seemingly decisive military victories of the Nazis in Europe, became the main collaborators throughout the occupation of Belgium. At first, the Germans were highly suspicious of the Belgians and the feeling was widely mutual. When, in January 1941, Degrelle delivered a speech in Liege which ended with a spirited 'Heil Hitler', General Eggert Reeder, head of the military administration (*Militarverwaltung*) in Brussels stated in a report to Berlin that Degrelle's allegiance was misleading and the man himself was an unreliable charlatan. The distrust remained until the end. The Rexists were never entrusted with political power; a few crumbs were tossed in the way of minor posts in the civic administration.

In the battle theatres of the Eastern Front, things were different. The opening of the German attack on Russia afforded the Rexists the opportunity to form *Legion Wallonien* as a voluntary military unit. From then on, total collaboration was advocated and in January 1943, Degrelle announced his wholesale support for the integration of the French-speaking Belgians, proclaiming: 'We are a Germanic race calling for integration into an expanded German empire.' The higher reaches of the German élite gave its backing, most notably Hitler himself, who lavished praise on the Belgian, proclaiming: 'If I had a son, I would wish him to be like you.' Such high esteem was expressed with the bestowal of the Knight's Cross of the Iron Cross, followed by the Oak Leaves, the latter making Degrelle, in August 1944, the 355th recipient. But by this stage of the war, this cut little ice with the Belgian people. Support for the

Rexists dwindled, their survival harried by constant attacks from the Resistance.

After the breakout from the Korsun pocket on the Eastern Front, Degrelle returned to Belgium, determined to talk up what he saw as triumphant resistance within the pocket. A spectacular, stage-managed parade through the streets of Charleroi and Brussels on 1 April was mounted by the men of *Wallonien*, who were by then severely depleted in number. In attendance were *SS-Leibstandarte Adolf Hitler* and its leader Sepp Dietrich. Incidentally, Degrelle had to borrow armour and other material from the *Leibstandarte*, so as to dress the parade convincingly. The German language radio in Belgium proclaimed:

'Leon Degrelle, standing on a tank, passed through at Charleroi, saluting the crowd with raised arm. The sight of the columns of the Legionnaires with the tricolour decorated with the Cherkassy badge, moved the huge crowd deeply. On the Place de l'Hotel de Ville, decorations were awarded to 150 men who distinguished themselves on the Eastern Front.'

In Brussels, with the newsreel cameras turning, Degrelle was seen smiling broadly as, accompanied by his young children, he rode on a tank at the head of his men. The crowd, consisting mainly of Rexists and their families, cheered him on. Then came a defiant peroration: 'We were a battalion and we became a brigade. Tomorrow we will be a division.' But any talk of tomorrow was pure illusion. The sweepings of the Walloon, Flemish and French SS divisions had been hastily assembled as the 'SS Army Corps West' to fight in the path of the Soviet advance into Pomerania. It was a pathetic affair. An engagement with the Red Army around Stettin resulted in heavy casualties with the strength of the 'Corps' cut to just 700 men.

Yet Degrelle, in the tradition of the true fanatic, refused to believe in the defeat of Germany. When the German armies launched their surprise short-lived offensive in the Belgian Ardennes during December

Left: Havalt Nugiseks, a *Waffen-SS* volunteer. As well as his Iron Cross First and Second Class, and an Infantry Assault Badge, he wears a ceremonial dagger hanging from his belt.

Right: A Dutch *Obersturmbannführer* **(Lieutentant-Colonel), commander of a regiment of the** *Legion Nederland***, takes care to duck as he moves down a trench on the Eastern Front.**

1944, he rushed to join them. He would, he declared, be the first Belgian to enter 'liberated Brussels' at the head of his *Comite de Liberation Walloon*. But such a committee in reality consisted merely of Degrelle himself and two of his colleagues. All hopes of success were now dwindling rapidly. By mid-April 1945, the Walloon survivors were all but annihilated on the west bank of the Oder; the remnants of the unit were then hastily evacuated by sea to Copenhagen.

But Degrelle still clutched at straws, pondering upon a scheme whereby his skeleton force of Rexists would join up with the thinning legions of the SS to form some sort of joint resistance group within Germany. On a road at Malente, near Kiel, he had an encounter with Himmler, still officially his chief. However, this was no longer the *Reichsführer-SS* of former days. Himmler, according to Degrelle's later account, was polite but evinced little interest, suggesting that the best course was to take charge of the *Waffen-SS* remnants at Copenhagen. Proceedings were interrupted by an air raid and the two men parted, leaving Himmler to make his way to an imaginary safe haven at Flensburg. Degrelle's dream collapsed. Next, he canvassed the Norwegian traitor Vidkun Quisling who appeared equally a busted flush. Degrelle, seeing no reason to offer himself for slaughter, took a private aircraft belonging to Hitler's Minister for War Production, Albert Speer, and which had been offered to Quisling should he wish to escape to Spain. The plane crash-landed on the beach at San Sebastian. Degrelle, half-drowned, crawled ashore with a broken collarbone and a wrenched ankle.

Successive attempts by Belgian governments to secure his extradition came to nothing in the face of constant stonewalling by his mentor, Spain's General Franco. To return home was out of the question; Degrelle had been sentenced to death *in absentia*. When the sentence expired in 1964 it was extended for a further 10 years by special decree. By then he was a Spanish citizen, sporting for the time being the name of Leon Jose de Ramirez Reina. He claimed later to have survived several kidnapping attempts, and for a while laid low, notably in 1961 after the unmasking of Adolf Eichmann. He claimed that at moments of danger there was always a police bodyguard on hand. He claimed: 'For 18 months I stayed in the homes of about a dozen high-ranking army officers while they mounted an apparently intensive but unsuccessful search operation.'

As unrepentant as ever, he was soon addressing fascist rallies in Spain and continuing to insist that the Jews who had died at Auschwitz and Dachau had been the victims of Allied bombing. In the 1980s the French-speaking channel of the Belgian television service decided to run three lengthy programmes on Degrelle and his wartime collaboration. This led to bitter protests from organizations of resistance fighters and survivors, particularly when it was learnt that the interviews had been filmed some years earlier but the authorities had then judged it impossible to show them. Degrelle was grilled in an hour of detailed exchanges with Maurice de Wilde, a specialist on the record of wartime collaboration. Degrelle refuted documentary evidence from SS headquarters in Berlin that he had been willing, not only to raise volunteers to fight 'the Godless Communists in the east', but also effectively hand over both the Walloon and Flemish regions in Belgium as a virtual German protectorate. Such an allegation, Degrelle insisted, was 'absolute rubbish'. He further claimed that reference to the 'Reich' in those documents referred, not to a German Reich, but to 'a union of Western European peoples, each guarding its own proper identity, an idea which I have always defended'. Confronted by transcripts of his own speeches in which he referred to the French-speaking Walloons 'as part of the great Germanic community', Degrelle stated that, until the early Middle Ages, Wallonia was part of the German empire which Charlemagne had founded. He also claimed that stressing these historical parallels had helped to win protection for his 4000 Wallonian-SS volunteers.

Over the years Degrelle thrived as a businessman, involved, ironically, in the building of military bases for the American armed forces as well as the running of a string of laundries. In his hilltop villa at Torreblanca, near Fuengirola, he cheerfully held court to anyone who would listen, readily granted interviews in a study crammed with books, video cassettes and memorabilia. A photograph exists of him strutting proudly in his old uniform as an SS-Standartenführer (Colonel). Indeed, he once appeared at a wedding in full Nazi regalia, including the decorations he had been awarded by Hitler. The Walloon flag remained his most cherished possession. The Belgians did their utmost to prevent Degrelle's supporters from travelling to Spain for his funeral, following his death in hospital in Malaga on 31 March 1994 at the age of 87. Some revisionist literature

still champions him. The introduction to a recent new translation of his book *The Eastern Front* refers to 'a public figure who for over 50 years has been in his native country, Belgium and abroad, one of the most admired as well as one of the most reviled and traduced figures of the century, long slandered by distortion'. By all accounts, Degrelle himself remained unperturbed. Not long before the end he was asked if he had any regrets about the past. He replied: 'Only that we lost.'

JOSEF MENGELE

Josef Mengele was born in Gunzburg in 1911. His solidly prosperous middle-class parents were devout Roman Catholics. He joined the youth wing of the nationalist paramilitary *Stahlhelm* at the age of 19. A natural progression was the rising Nazi party and the ranks of the *Sturm Abteilung* (SA – Storm Troopers). However, Mengele was prevented by ill-health from active membership of the Storm Troopers and so opted to complete his education.

He gained his Doctorate from the University of Munich. The choice of subject was significant: the study of anthropology and genetics. At the start of 1937, he was appointed a research assistant at the Third Reich Institute for Heredity, Biology and Racial Purity at the University of Frankfurt. From there he gained his medical degree. His openly declared racial beliefs – the superiority of the Aryan race and the conviction that Germany had a particular destiny in achieving it – were soon attracting the attention of leading academics sympathetic to the Nazis. It was inevitable that he should seek to join the SS, which saw itself as the supreme guardian of the nation's racial purity. Mengele also joined the *Nationalsozialistische Arztebund*, the *Schutzstaffel's* medical association, which was an essential requirement for any doctor seeking advancement.

With the approach of war, Josef Mengele joined the future *Waffen-SS*, doing his basic training with the *Wehrmacht*, having previously served in the Tyrol with a mountain light infantry regiment. In August 1940, he gained the rank of *SS-Untersturmführer* (Lieutenant) and in the following year was posted to the Ukraine. It was here that he first saw action and was awarded the

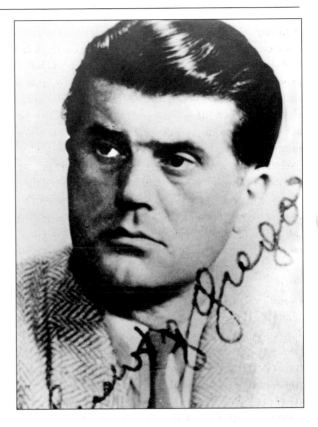

Right: Dr Josef Mengele, the 'Angel of Death', who briefly served with Wiking before moving to Auschwitz concentration camp. This photograph is taken post war and shows him using the alias Ludwig Gregor.

Iron Cross Second Class. Previous to the Russian posting, however, he was in occupied Poland, attached to the Genealogical Section of the Race and Settlement Office, under the direct control of Heinrich Himmler. Here teams of SS doctors were assigned to examine the racial suitability of the future inhabitants of German-conquered territories.

Mengele joined the *Wiking* Division medical corps in January 1942 and was highly commended for his action in saving the lives of two of his comrades, trapped in a blazing tank, following the reconquest of Rostov in 1942. The wounds that he later received put paid to his career in the *Waffen-SS*. But for the rest of his life, *SS-Haupsturmführer* (Captain) Josef Mengele would remain especially proud of the Black Badge of the Wounded and the Medal for the Care of the German People which he had been awarded in addition to the Iron Cross First Class.

During his time at Auschwitz concentration camp, where he arrived in May 1943 and where he became chief medical officer, he constantly boasted that he was the only doctor with such an array of decorations. At Auschwitz, one of the cradles of the Holocaust, Mengele, dubbed 'The Angel of Death', gave full rein to his twisted racial ambitions, conducting bogus medical experiments on twins, dwarfs, giants and cripples. Apart from these activities, Mengele was chiefly to be remembered for his arrogant way of classifying newly arrived prisoners; he would stand looking them over, indicating with either a flick of his thumb or the movement of his cane which of those in front of him were to become slave labourers.

At the approach of the end of the war, Mengele exchanged his SS uniform for that of an ordinary German soldier but nevertheless he was arrested and soon placed in a prisoner-of-war camp near Munich which was run by the Americans. By a cruel irony, unlike most members of the *Waffen-SS*, Mengele had – possibly for reasons of his vanity – not permitted the

standard tattoo of his blood type to be placed on his chest beneath his arm. This was a momentous decision as it would save him from automatic arrest as a war criminal at the end of World War II.

Although he was soon the object of a massive manhunt across the whole of Europe, Mengele managed to lie low for four years. In 1949 he slipped out of Germany and made his way to Argentina. During the next four decades – under a string of aliases – he lived in several locations in South America.

By early 1979, Mengele was living in Brazil under the name of Wolfgang Gerhard. On the late afternoon of 7 February of the same year, at Bertioga Beach in Embu, he drowned. It is reported that he had suffered a stroke while swimming in the Atlantic. Any doubts over the identity of the man who was buried as Wolfgang Gerhard were finally resolved when the remains were exhumed by a team of scientists in 1992 and were eventually identified to be those of the notorious Josef Mengele.

LINEAGE

Nordische Division *(Nr.5),* 1940

SS-Division Germania (mot), 1940

SS-Division Wiking, 1941

SS-Panzergrenadier-Division Wiking, 1942

5.SS-Panzer-Division Wiking, 1943

DIVISIONAL COMMANDERS

12.1.40–1.5.43
SS-*Obergruppenführer und General der Waffen-SS* **Felix Steiner**

1.5.43–6.8.44
SS-*Obergruppenführer und General der Waffen-SS* **Herbert Gille**

6.8.44–?.8.44
SS-*Oberführer* **Edmund Deisenhofer**

?.8.44–9.10.44
SS-*Standartenführer* **Rudolf Mühlenkamp**

9.10.44–5.5.45
SS-*Oberführer* **Karl Ullrich**

Legion Wallonien Commanders

?.6.43–20.2.44
SS-*Sturmbannführer* **Lucien Lippert**

20.2.44–8.5.45
SS-*Obersturmbannführer* **Leon Degrelle**

WAFFEN-SS RANKS AND THEIR ENGLISH EQUIVALENTS

SS-Schütze	Private	**SS-Hauptsturmführer**	Captain
SS-Oberschütze	Senior Private, attained after six months' service	**SS-Sturmbannführer**	Major
		SS-Oberbannsturmführer	Lieutenant-Colonel
SS-Sturmmann	Lance-Corporal	**SS-Standartenführer**	Colonel
SS-Rottenführer	Corporal	**SS-Oberführer**	Senior Colonel
SS-Unterscharführer	Senior Corporal /Lance-Sergeant	**SS-Brigadeführer und Generalmajor der Waffen-SS**	Major-General
SS-Scharführer	Sergeant	**SS-Gruppenführer und Generalleutnant der Waffen-SS**	Lieutenant-General
SS-Oberscharführer	Staff Sergeant		
SS-Hauptscharführer	Warrant Officer	**SS-Obergruppenführer und General der Waffen-SS**	General
SS-Sturmscharführer	Senior Warrant Officer after 15 years' service	**SS-Oberstgruppenführer und Generaloberst der Waffen-SS**	Colonel-General
SS-Untersturmführer	Second Lieutenant		
SS-Obersturmführer	First Lieutenant	**Reichsführer-SS**	(no English equivalent)

		WAR SERVICE		
Date	**Corps**	**Army**	**Army Group**	**Area**
3.41	*Wehrkreis VII*			Germany
4.41	XXIV	11th Army	C	Germany
5.41	*Wehrkreis V*	2nd Panzer Group	-	Germany
6.41–8.41	XIV	1st Panzer Group	South	Tarnopol, Kiev
9.41–10.41	III	1st Panzer Group	South	Kiev, Rostov
11.41–5.42	XIV	1st Pz. Army	South	Mius (Taganrog)
6.42	XIV	-	South	Mius (Taganrog)
7.42	LVII	-	South	South Russia
8.42	LVII	1st Pz. Army	A	Caucasus
9.42	LVII	17th Army	A	Caucasus
10.42–11.42	LII	1st Pz. Army	A	Caucasus
12.42	III	1st Pz. Army	A	Caucasus
1.43–2.43	LVII	4th Pz. Army	Don	Manytsch
3.43–5.43	XXXX	1st Pz. Army	South	Isyum, Kharkov
6.43	XXIV	1st Pz. Army	South	Isyum, Kharkov
7.43	Reserve	1st Pz. Army	South	Isyum, Kharkov
8.43	XXXX and LVII	1st Pz. Army	South	Isyum, Kharkov
9.43–12.43	III	8th Army	South	Dniepr
1.44–3.44	XI	8th Army	South	Cherkassy
4.44	LVI	2nd Army	Centre	Kovel
5.44–7.44	refitting	-	Centre	Heidelager
8.44–12.44	IV SS	9th Army	Centre	Modlin
1.45	Reserve	6th Army	South	Hungary
2.45–4.45	IV SS	6th Army	South	Hungary
5.45	*IV SS*	-	Ostmark	Graz, Austria

ORDER OF BATTLE MAY 1944

Divisional Staff

Divisional Escort Company
Motorcycle Platoon (6 x LMGs)
Self Propelled Flak Battery (4 x 20mm (0.78in)
  guns)
Self Propelled Anti-Tank Platoon (3 x LMGs &
  3 x 75mm (2.95in) Pak 40)
Infantry Gun Platoon (2 x 75mm (2.95in) leIG)
Mixed Panzergrenadier Platoon (4 x HMGs,
  6 x LMGs, & 2 x 81mm (3.2in) mortars)

5th SS Panzer Regiment
Regimental Staff

I Panzer Battalion (I–IV Companies)
  (Mk V Panthers)
  1 Panzer Maintenance Platoon

II Panzer Battalion (V–VIII Companies)
  (Mk IV Panzers)
  1 Panzer Maintenance Company

9th SS Panzergrenadier Regiment Germania
  Regimental Staff

I Battalion
  I–III Companies (4 x HMGs, 18 x LMGs, 2 x
    81mm (3.2in) mortars & 2 x flamethrowers)
  IV Company
    1 Mortar Platoon (2 x LMGs and 4 x 120mm
      (4.72in) mortars)
    1 Panzerjäger Platoon (3 x LMGs &
      3 x 75mm (2.95in) Pak 40)
    2 Infantry Gun Sections (2 x LMG &
      4 x 75mm (2.95in) leIG)

II Battalion (VI–X Companies)
  (same as I Battalion)

III (Halftrack) Battalion (XI–XV Companies)
  I–III (Halftrack) Companies (4 x HMGs,
    40 x LMGs, 2 x 81mm (3.2in) mortars,
    2 x flamethrowers, 7 x 20mm (0.78in) guns &
    2 x 75mm (2.95in) guns)

IV Company
  1 Pioneer Platoon (13 x LMGs &
    6 x flamethrowers)
  1 Infantry Gun Section (1 x LMG & 2 x 75mm
    (2.95in) leIG)
  1 Panzerjäger Platoon
    (8 x LMGs & 3 x 75mm (2.95in) Pak 40)
  1 Gun Platoon
    (8 x LMGs & 6 x 75mm (2.95in) guns)

XVI (Self-propelled Flak) Company (12 x 20mm
  (0.78in) & 4 x LMGs)
XVII (Self-propelled Infantry Gun) Company
  (6 x 150mm (5.9in) sIG & 8 x LMGs)
XVIII (mot) Pioneer Company (2 x HMGs,
  12 x LMGs, 6 x flamethrowers & 2 x 81mm
  (3.2in) mortars)

10th SS Panzergrenadier Regiment Westland
  same as 9th SS Panzergrenadier Regiment

5th SS Reconnaissance Battalion
Battalion Staff
Heavy Platoon (6 x SdKfz 234/3 with 75mm
  (2.95in) KwK & 6 x LMGs)
1 Armored Car Company (18 x 20mm (0.78in) &
  24 x LMGs)
1 (Halftrack) Armored Car Company (16 x 20mm
  (0.78in) & 25 x LMGs)
2 (Halftrack) Companies (49 x LMGs, 2 x 81mm
  (3.2in) mortars & 3 x 75mm (2.95in) guns)
1 (Halftrack) Company
  1 Pioneer Platoon (13 x LMGs &
    6 x flamethrowers)
  1 Panzerjäger Platoon (8 x LMGs & 3 x 75mm
    (2.95in) Pak 40)
  1 Infantry Gun Section (2 x 75mm (2.95in) leIG
    & 4 x LMGs)
  1 Gun Section (8 x LMGs & 6 x 75mm (2.95in)
    guns)
1 (mot) Reconnaissance Supply Column (3 x
  LMGs)

5th SS Panzerjäger Battalion
Battalion Staff

3 Self Propelled Panzerjäger Companies
(14 x 75mm (2.95in) Pak 40 & 14 x LMGs each)

5th SS Panzer Artillery Regiment
1 Regimental Staff & Staff Battery (2 x LMGs)
1 Self Propelled Flak Battery (4 x quad 20mm
(0.78in) guns & 2 x LMGs)

I (Self-propelled) Battalion
Staff & (Self-propelled) Staff Battery (3 x LMGs
& 3 x 20mm (0.78in) guns)
2 Self Propelled leFH Batteries (6 x 105mm
(4.1in) leFH SdKfz 124 Wespe each)
1 Self Propelled sFH Battery (6 x 150mm (5.9in)
sFH SdKfz 165 Hummel)

II Battalion
Staff & Staff Battery (3 x LMGs & 3 x 20mm
(0.78in) guns)
2 (motZ) Batteries (6 x 105mm (4.1in) leFH &
2 x LMGs each)

III Battalion same as II Battalion

IV Battalion
Staff & Staff Battery (3 x LMGs & 3 x 20mm
(0.78in) guns)
2 (motZ) Batteries (6 x 150mm (5.9in) sFH &
2 x LMGs each)
1 (motZ) Battery (6 x 105mm (4.1in) sK 18/40
guns & 2 x LMGs each)

5th SS Flak Battalion
Staff & Staff Battery
3 (motZ) heavy Flak Batteries (4 x 88mm (3.45in),
3 x 20mm (0.78in) & 2 x MGs each)
1 (motZ) Medium Flak Batteries (9 x 37mm
(1.45in) & 4 x LMGs each)
1 (motZ) Searchlight Platoon (4 x 600mm
(23.6in) searchlights)

5th SS Panzer Pioneer Battalion
Staff (2 x LMGs)
1 (Halftrack) Pioneer Company (2 x HMGs,
46 x LMGs, 3 x heavy anti-tank rifles, 2 x 81mm
(3.2in) mortars & 6 x flamethrowers)

2 (mot) Pioneer Companies (2 x HMGs,
18 x LMGs, 2 x 81mm (3.45in) mortars &
6 x flamethrowers)
1 (mot) Heavy Panzer Bridging Train (5 x LMGs)
1 (mot) Light Panzer Bridging Train (3 x LMGs)

5th SS Panzer Signals Battalion
1 Panzer Telephone Company (14 x LMGs)
1 Panzer Radio Company (20 x LMGs)
1 (mot) Signals Supply Column (1 x LMG)

5th SS Feldersatz Battalion
5 Companies

5th SS Supply Troop
I–VII 5th SS (mot) 120 ton Transportation
Companies (8 x LMGs each)
5/5th SS (mot) 20 ton Light Flak Supply Column
5th SS (mot) Workshop Company (4 x LMGs)
5th SS (mot) Supply Company (8 x LMGs)

5th SS Truck Park
1/,2/,3/5th SS (mot) Maintenance Companies
(4 x LMGs)
5th SS (mot) 75 ton Heavy Maintenance Supply
Column

Medical
1/,2/5th SS (mot) Medical Companies (2 x LMGs
each)
1/,2/,3/5th SS Ambulances

Administration
5th SS (mot) Bakery Company (6 x LMGs)
5th SS (mot) Butcher Company (6 x LMGs)
5th SS (mot) Divisional Administration Platoon
(2 x LMGs)
5th SS (mot) Military Police Troop (5 platoons)
(15 x LMGs)
5th SS (mot) Field Post Office (2 x LMGs)

WAFFEN-SS DIVISIONS 1939–45

Title (and nominal divisional strength at the beginning of 1945)	Granted Divisional Status	Knight's Crosses Awarded
1st SS-Panzer Division *Leibstandarte-SS Adolf Hitler* (22,000)	1942	58
2nd SS-Panzer Division *Das Reich* (18,000)	1939	69
3rd SS-Panzer Division *Totenkopf* (15,400)	1939	47
4th SS-Panzergrenadier Division *Polizei* (9,000)	1939	25
5th SS-Panzer Division *Wiking* (14,800)	1940	55
6th SS-Gebirgs Division *Nord* (15,000)	1941	4
7th SS-Freiwilligen Gebirgs Division *Prinz Eugen* (20,000)	1942	6
8th SS-Kavallerie Division *Florian Geyer* (13,000)	1942	22
9th SS-Panzer Division *Hohenstaufen* (19,000)	1943	12
10th SS-Panzer Division *Frundsberg* (15,500)	1943	13
11th SS-Freiwilligen Panzergrenadier Division *Nordland* (9,000)	1943	25
12th SS-Panzer Division *Hitlerjugend* (19,500)	1943	14
13th Waffen Gebirgs Division der SS *Handschar* (12,700)	1943	4
14th Waffen Grenadier Division der SS (22,000)	1943	1
15th Waffen Grenadier Division der SS (16,800)	1943	3
16th SS-Panzergrenadier Division *Reichsführer-SS* (14,000)	1943	1
17th SS-Panzergrenadier Division *Götz von Berlichingen* (3500)	1943	4
18th SS-Freiwilligen Panzergrenadier Division *Horst Wessel* (11,000)	1944	2
19th Waffen Grenadier Division der SS (9000)	1944	12
20th Waffen Grenadier Division der SS (15,500)	1944	5
21st Waffen Gebirgs Division der SS *Skanderbeg* (5000)	1944	0
22nd SS-Freiwilligen Kavallerie Division *Maria Theresa* (8000)	1944	6
23rd Waffen Gebirgs Division der SS *Kama* (disbanded late 1944, number '23' given to next division)	1944	0
23rd SS-Freiwilligen Panzergrenadier Division *Nederland* (6000)	1945	19
24th Waffen Gebirgskarstjäger Division der SS (3000)	1944	0
25th Waffen Grenadier Division der SS *Hunyadi* (15,000)	1944	0
26th Waffen Grenadier Division der SS (13,000)	1945	0
27th SS-Freiwilligen Grenadier Division *Langemarck* (7000)	1944	1
28th SS-Freiwilligen Grenadier Division *Wallonien* (4000)	1944	3
29th Waffen Grenadier Division der SS (disbanded late 1944, number '29' given to next division)	1944	0
29th Waffen Grenadier Division der SS (15,000)	1945	0
30th Waffen Grenadier Division der SS (4500)	1945	0

31st SS-Freiwilligen Grenadier Division *Böhmen-Mähren* (11,000)	1945	0
32nd SS-Freiwilligen Grenadier Division *30 Januar* (2000)	1945	0
33rd Waffen *Kavallerie* Division der SS (destroyed soon after formation, number '33' given to next division)	1945	0
33rd Waffen Grenadier Division der SS *Charlemagne* (7000)	1945	2
34th SS-Freiwilligen Grenadier Division *Landstorm Nederland* (7000)	1945	3
35th SS-Polizei Grenadier Division (5000)	1945	0
36th Waffen Grenadier Division der SS (6000)	1945	1
37th SS-Freiwilligen Kavallerie Division *Lützow* (1000)	1945	0
38th SS-Grenadier Division *Nibelungen* (1000)	1945	0

BIBLIOGRAPHY

Ailsby, Christopher, *Hell on the Eastern Front: The Waffen-SS War in Russia 1941–1945,* Spellmount Ltd, 1998.

Barker, A. J., *Waffen-SS At War,* Ian Allan Ltd, 1982.

Blandford, Edmund L., *Hitler's Second Army: The Waffen-SS,* Airlife, 1994.

Butler, Rupert, *The Black Angels,* Arrow Books, 1989.

Butler, Rupert, *Hitler's Jackals,* Leo Cooper, 1998.

Carrell, Paul, *Hitler's War on Russia: 1943–1944,* Schiffer Publishing Ltd, 1994.

Clark, Allan, *Barbarossa: The Russo–German Conflict 1941–1945,* Hutchinson, 1965.

Conway, Martin, *Collaboration in Belgium,* Yale University Press, 1993.

Fosten, D. S. V. & Marrion, R. J., *Waffen-SS: Its Uniforms, Insignia and Equipment 1938–1945,* Almark Publishing Co Ltd, 1971.

Degrelle, Leon, *Campaign in Russia,* Institute for Historical Review, 1985.

Gilbert, Martin, *Second World War,* George Weidenfeld & Nicholson, 1989.

Guderian, General Heinz, *Panzer Leader,* Futura, 1952.

History of the Second World War, various volumes, Purnell & Sons, 1966.

Littlejohn, David, *The Patriotic Traitors: A History of Collaboration in German Occupied Europe,* Doubleday, 1972.

Messenger, Charles, *The Last Prussian: A Biography of Field Marshal Gerd von Rundstedt 1875–1953,* Brasseys, 1991.

Mollo, Andrew, *Uniforms of the SS, Volume 7,* Historic Research Unit, 1976.

Neumann, Peter, *Other Men's Graves,* Weidenfeld & Nicholson, 1958.

Panzer Grenadiere der Panzerdivision Wiking *Im Bild,* Munin Verlag GMBH, 1984.

Posner, Gerald J. & Ware, John, *Mengele: The Complete Story,* Queen Anne Press, 1986.

Quarrie, Bruce, *Hitler's Samurai,* Patrick Stephens, 1983.

Quarrie, Bruce, *Weapons of the Waffen-SS,* Patrick Stephens, 1988.

Reitlinger, Gerald, *The SS: Alibi of a Nation, 1939–1945,* William Heinemann Ltd, 1956.

Stein, George H, *The Waffen-SS: Hitler's Elite Guard At War,* Cornell University, 1966.

Strassner, Peter, *European Volunteers,* J. J. Fedorowicz Publishing, 1988.

Sydnor, Jr., Charles W., *Soldiers of Destruction,* Princetown University Press, 1977.

Toland, John, *The Last 100 Days,* Arthur Barker, 1965.

Werth, Alexander, *Russia at War,* Barrie & Rockliff, 1964.

Williamson, Gordon, *The Blood Soaked Soil,* Blitz Editions, 1997.

Williamson, Gordon, *Loyalty Is My Honour,* Brown Books, 1995.

Williamson, Gordon, *The SS: Hitler's Instrument of Terror,* Sidgwick & Jackson, 1994.

INDEX